Air to Ground

A Guide for Pilots to the World of Air Traffic Control
And Aviation Weather

Rose Marie Kern

Air To Ground
A Guide for Pilots to the World of Air Traffic Control
All Right Reserved.
Copyright © 2017 Rose Marie Kern
www.rosemariekern.com

Warning and Disclaimer
Every effort has been made to make this book as complete and as accurate as possible, but no warranty or fitness is implied. The information provided is on an "as is" basis. The author and the publisher shall have neither liability nor responsibility to any person or entity with respect to any loss or damages arising from the information contain in this book.

For information about buying this title in bulk quantities or for special sales opportunities (which may include electronic versions) please contact our corporate sales department at solarranch@swcp.com

Solar Ranch Publishing   1655 Flora Vista DR. SW   Albuquerque, NM 87105

ISBN: 978-0-9985725-0-5
Library of Congress control number 1-4128274051

Table of Contents

Introduction

The relationship between pilots and air traffic control personnel has never been cavalier. There is an invisible wall that exists — a disembodied voice that carries instructions phrased in officially sanctioned terminology which is both reassuringly familiar and yet remote and impersonal.

Air Traffic Controllers are distant authoritative dictators whose main purpose in life is to keep pilots from killing themselves and others by telling them where to go. Behind the confident decisive voices you hear over the radios are people who go through some intensive training in order to get a job that pays well and commands respect.

In the days of the old FAA Flight Services — where there was a station at airports of any size at all, the pilots could at least meet and talk with someone who represented that faceless megalith known as the Federal Aviation Administration (FAA). Consolidation of those small stations into the large automated stations relegated most pilot contacts to phones and frequencies.

During my tenure with the FAA, and later with Lockheed Martin, I worked in the Air Route Traffic Control Center, the Tower, and the Flight Service environments. I was hired about two years after the infamous Air Traffic Control (ATC) strike of 1981 had decimated the ranks of Controllers across the country.

For over 32 years I have enjoyed working with pilots – new pilots, old pilots, airline pilots, military pilots, balloon pilots…all of them have needs that are similar, yet require tailoring to their flight and type aircraft.

New pilots are all excited about learning how to fly – a daunting task in and of itself, yet in the midst of trying to remember how many degrees of flap are needed to take off, he suddenly has to juggle a microphone and recall not only what he has to tell a tower or Unicom, but how to say it correctly.

Although there are government-composed manuals such as the Airman's Information Manual and the Notices to Airmen that pilots must reference during their careers, I have noticed that much of ATC is still a mystery to the flying community. The pilot knows what he is supposed to do, but not why he needs to do it. Frequently he or she does not realize that there are options that may make planning and executing a flight easier for both the pilot and ATC.

The articles I have written for magazines and newsletters over the past 10 years were designed to fill that gap. Pilots have asked me questions related to weather briefings, IFR clearances, search and rescue, NOTAMs, PIREPs and generally how to work with ATC to get what they need.

The public does not generally make jokes about ATC, but believe it or not ATC controllers do have a sense of humor. So you will also find that there are aviation jokes, stories and other amusing anecdotes included in the manuscript. These stories are the ones we swap on the ATC side of the microphone. Mind you, they are ones that have passed through the grapevine, so their validity is questionable, and the names and some locations have been changed to protect the guilty. There is also a lot of general aviation humor that I have collected.

This book is not an official publication of the Federal Aviation Administration and not officially approved by them or any other company working with them…it is mostly my observations and insights. I do cite references to other sources that are sanctioned, some of which are noted in the articles and some are listed in the appendix.

The book was written primarily because I have had many pilots request a compilation of the articles I have written. The data has been updated as times have changed…for instance, I wrote several articles about Flight Watch and Airport Advisories – both services no longer exist and are only mentioned here in a historical context.

I have truly enjoyed working with pilots, for every one of you that has had me tearing my hair out, there has been one that made me laugh. Thank you for the FAM (familiarization) flights, thank you for making it possible for me to have a job that helped a single Mom raise her kids alone.

Hope you like the book.

Rose Marie Kern

WWW.FLY-LOW.com

Forward

Written by Ralph McCormick

Managing Editor, *Fly-Low Magazine*

Many years ago, I received an email from a reader who suggested I contact a writer to see if she would be interested in writing for my publication. Believe it or not, I get lots of that that kind of request, but this one seemed different. The guy was familiar with her work; spoke highly of her. From past experience, I knew that all writers are not created equal; therefore, I was skeptical about contacting her. The reader was very adamant that I should contact her. Thus, I did!

That was eight years ago, I contacted Rose Marie Kern via email. We corresponded through email; a document was sent to me for review and it looked good. Her credentials appeared very solid, her background of experience both in air traffic control and as a writer showed us she was familiar with what our readers needed…in other words, Rose was right down FLY-LOW's "alley"; able to bring knowledge from the FAA to our readers in a personal way. This is what Rose achieves and she does it very well; turning the tough, hard balled, sometimes (mostly often) confusing FAA information in to "pilot speak."

As our years of working together mounted, it was easy to see that her talent was infinite and the readers loved her. We receive many e-mails requesting more from her, and adulations for her prose. There is no doubt that Rose can disperse words from the FAA in a manner which pilots do understand. It is important to realize that there is a vast abyss between the FAA Regs and the average pilot. What we have through Rose is the catalyst with which to convert and provide a bridge between the FAA regs and pilots. She does it with class and explicit common sense.

I believe that it was my good fortune to have Rose providing articles for my publication. So much has changed over the past thirty years. When I first started flying, Flight Service Stations were on airports, often maintaining the Unicom frequency. Upon landing, we could just walk into the office for a "complete personal" briefing. Today, FSS is no longer located at airports in individual states. They are located in somewhere in America with radar, maps, and info about all states. Basically, it is a lot more impersonal and the briefer may not be as aware of your state as they were they were in the "old" days. Rose's many years with the FAA has provided her with the capability to share to readers her experiences.

What we find in Rose's columns is a bit of humor from pilots and FAA staff. The truth can be far more humorous than fiction. Sometime ago, I suggested that she compose a book from the monthly articles along with articles from her archives. The idea stayed on her mind and now we have her words in book format for all of us to enjoy and learn.

ACKNOWLEDGEMENTS

I am grateful to all the pilots and controllers I have worked with over the years who have given me the opportunity to work in this amazing industry and accumulate 32 years' worth of the stories and general information that are contained herein.

Many thanks to Cindy Willman, David Edwards, Randy Crawford, Dennis Livesay, Steve Prout and the others of my co-workers who have looked over my notes to check for accuracy, and contributed incidents from their careers to add to the interesting incidents I speak about. Thank you to Jack Hickman of the Albuquerque Experimental Aircraft Association who got me started in writing for aviation periodicals and the Southwest Writer's Association for all the workshops and advice on writing. Also I want to thank Jim Hartley, the editor of *America's Flyways* for boosting me into national publication, Ralph McCormick of *Fly Low* magazine and pilot/writer Jim Trusty for a lot of ego lifting and encouragement.

Most especially, thanks to my best friend, Tom, for being my first line copy editor, advisor, and enthusiastic supporter.

~~~ *Rose Marie Kern*

Publications

Each chapter in this book is the reposting of an article that was written by Rose Marie Kern and published nationally by one or more of the following:

Fly-Low Magazine

IFR Refresher Magazine

The Atlantic Flyer

America's Flyways Magazine

Plane and Pilot News

America's Flyways

EAA Chapter Newsletters

The FAA Intercom

Lockheed Martin's Flight Service Website

PilotsandWeather.com

Compilot.com

Cloudbouncer

Author's note: In cases where the original publisher posted the article online, they were frequently picked up by aviation magazines in other countries without permission of the author.

Chapter 1

The National Airspace System (NAS)

Today's National Airspace System may have begun small right after World War I, but over a relatively short time it grew into the largest, most respected aviation structure in the world. The NAS is not just about air traffic control, it is the rules and regulations that govern the aircraft, airports, airspace and all the people that work and play from the surface upwards.

- Air Traffic Control facilities – Towers, Centers, Flight Services
- Flight Standards inspectors
- FAA publications
- NAS information, rules and regulations for ATC and pilots
- Airport Facilities and Classes of airspace
- Anything that flys – aircraft, balloons, rockets, drones, etc…
- IFR, VFR and sectional charts
- Airways/Jet Routes, military operating areas.
- Navigational Aids – such as VORTACs, GPS, Satellite systems
- Restricted airspace procedures/Notices to Airmen
- Flow Control to and from busy airports
- Airway Facilities technicians
- Radio frequency and telephone line communications systems
- Computer technology and radar systems
- Administration by the Federal Aviation Administration (FAA)
- Congressional committee oversight

The NAS includes all types of aircraft from small private single engines to large air carriers to NASA rocketry. Dirigibles, hot air balloons, hang gliders, helicopters, parachute jumpers, drones, military jets…if it flies in the United States, it must comply with NAS requirements.

Since the end of World War I, aviation has grown to the point that on any given day there can be over 5,000 aircraft in U.S. skies at once.

Airspace is divided into classes, and the requirements for flying in each type varies. Classes A, B, C and D always require communication and clearance from an ATC facility, each has different requirements for the types of flight, aircraft and pilot certification allowed.

Class E airspace is general aviation's most precious resource – a place where pilots can fly without being in constant contact with air traffic. It is a pilot's version of being "off road", like speeding in an ATV across open desert.

Yet, even that contains areas where flight is limited or not allowed – restricted airspace. Restricted airspace can be surface based areas over protected people, places or facilities such as Los Alamos National labs, White Sands Missile range or the White House. It can be a temporary location over a forest fire or accident investigation area. It can also be blocks of airspace beginning above the ground where the military aircraft are practicing aerial combat maneuvers.

The NAS includes airport safety – the FAA works with managers to ensure runways are strong enough to support the repeated landings of whatever aircraft they serve. They inspect and monitor airport navigational aids, lighting, equipment, fuels, and frequencies.

In addition to the FAA, the NAS weaves other governmental elements into the tapestry of aviation. The National Weather Service has a branch devoted to aviation weather, the National Notices to Airmen (NOTAM) department is a division whose mission is to ensure pilots are informed about every NAS element that deviates from normal conditions. Many services related to the NAS are provided by private contractors.

The portions of the NAS we will concentrate on in this book is Air Traffic Control and services/elements that directly concern pilots, with emphasis on general aviation.

Airspace Classes

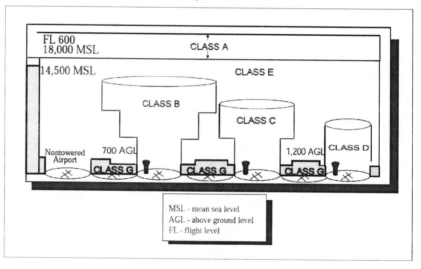

Chapter 2

Classes of Airspace

The air above the ground all over the U.S. is divided into classes of airspace. Each class has different rules based on the complexity and density of traffic. Let's start with defining what each class is and how to deal with it.

When building a mental picture of airspace, start with class E, as in Everywhere. Class E is what the United States started out with in the 1920s when there were no aircraft that flew very high and jet engines were yet to be invented. Class E has no restrictions and it is from the surface to 17,999 feet MSL throughout the U.S and within 12 miles of the shorelines. West of the Mississippi river there is still a great deal of CLASS E airspace where many pilots both domestic and foreign come to train and build their hours.

Once high performance aircraft began to enter the arena, it was determined that different rules were needed to accommodate them. Since these aircraft generally flew higher up, the airspace was divided by altitude. CLASS A airspace is the positive control area or PCA. It begins at 18,000FT MSL (FL180) and extends upwards to 60,000FT MSL or Flight level 6-0-0 (FL600). All aircraft flying at or above FL180 must be transponder equipped, on a flight plan, and talking to Air Traffic Control (ATC).

As some airspace, primarily around major airports, became more congested with aircraft accidents occurred more frequently, the FAA determined that all aircraft flying in certain areas should be under direct control. Procedures were developed to help controllers maintain separation even before there was radar. Of course, radar made it much easier to determine exactly where an aircraft was located. The airspace around the busy airports was designated B, C, or D depending on what level of traffic the airport served and what kinds of ATC services were available. The sizes of each of the classes of airspace vary, but here are the general rules.

CLASS B airspace – the busiest of the busiest. In general Class B airspace is from the surface to at least 10,000AGL. It is based at the airport and goes out to at least a 10 Nautical Mile radius at the surface upwards. However it does not form just a cylinder. Beginning at around 1,200FT AGL the airspace expands to a 20NM radius – following the aircrafts outbound or inbound pathways. It does not include the ground areas outside the 10NM radius so VFR aircraft can transit the lower altitudes without getting caught up in the major airport's traffic as long as they stay away from the inner area.

The airspace may expand again around 4,000FT and extend further up depending on the overall level of traffic being worked by ATC. Most books use the description of a standard wedding cake upside down to describe how the airspace expands with altitude. All Class B airspace is associated with an Approach Control or TRACON, however, the lateral limits of TRACON responsibility is not the same as the CLASS airspace. TRACONs may control the airspace over multiple airports, each of which is under a different CLASS of airspace

All aircraft operating in CLASS B airspace must be on a flight plan, have an ATC clearance, have a Mode C with altitude encoding transponder and operable radios. The pilot must either already have his private pilot's license

18

or if he is a student he must have met the criteria to attain one. An aircraft flying VFR must adhere to these rules. He can transit the airspace as long as he is in contact with the governing ATC facility.

CLASS C airspace is the next step down from CLASS B. These airports are still busy enough to require an approach control, but are not quite as large or complex. Their airspace usually only has two tiers. All aircraft, IFR or VFR, must have a 2 way radio and a transponder with altitude encoding.

When an airport has an Air Traffic Control Tower (ATCT) but no approach control, the airspace is CLASS D.   It is usually a 5NM radius of the airport surface to 2,500FT AGL.   Sometime there is a corridor that extends outwards for another 5NM lined up with the busiest runway to give inbound traffic more maneuvering area.

In CLASS A,B,C, and D airspace, aircraft are required to contact the controlling agency (ATCT or Center) prior to entering these areas, and abide by their instructions. The Airmen's Information Manual (AIM) available on the FAA's website   (www.faa.gov/publications) lists all airports that currently boast CLASS B and C airspace.

No ultralights, hot air balloons, or parachute jumping is allowed within CLASS A,B,C,or D airspace without special permission from ATC prior to flight.

An aircraft flying VFR and wanting to transit or enter the CLASS B,C, or D airspace must call the published ATC frequency at least 5 minutes before crossing the boundary and state its Aircraft Identification, position, altitude, transponder code, and intentions. (Land or transit).   If the controller states the aircraft ID back and the word "Standby", or some other instruction, then communication is established and the aircraft can continue inbound unless specifically told to remain outside of the airspace. If communication is not established the aircraft should stay clear of the airspace until it is.

Again, the data concerning the CLASS boundaries and altitudes here varies by airport. More specific information is available on aviation sectional, IFR Low Altitude and Terminal area charts. Do not confuse CLASS airspace with the boundaries of an Approach Control or TRACON—be sure to look that data up prior to flying in the area.

Chapter 3

Air Space Division and
Separation of ATC Duties

Tower? Center? Or Flight Service?

Do you know who the first Air Traffic Controller was? Wilbur Wright, as he yelled "It's clear - go ahead Orville!"

Although there are three divisions of Air Traffic Control, most people only see Towers – and from TV and movies they know about radar, but they think that if you are an Air Traffic Controller it follows that you must work at an airport.

21

New pilots are taught that there are three major divisions of Air Traffic – Air Route Traffic Control Centers (ARTCC or Center), Air Traffic Control Towers (ATCT or Tower) which may also have an Approach/ Departure Control, and Flight Service Stations (FSS)– also known as Radio. Improved technology is changing these definitions and many Approach/Departure control facilities are completely separate from the Towers, and not necessary located at the airport they serve.

The Airspace above us in the United States is divided up into areas that are either controlled or uncontrolled. Uncontrolled airspace is everything that is not designated as something else, and it is one of the most precious things that pilots here in the United States have access to.

The largest areas of uncontrolled airspace are out west – which is where students come from all over the world to learn to fly, and many European pilots come to build their hours so they can apply for jobs with air taxis and airlines once they return home.

The United States was the first country to develop a National Airspace System (NAS), and in addition to our own people, the Air Traffic Control academy in Oklahoma City has taught hundreds of classes in the basics of the NAS to representatives from other countries who then take that knowledge home. By doing this, the U.S. not only promotes a system whereby any pilot knows what to expect no matter where they fly, but they also have established that English is the language of Aviation throughout the free world.

Before the existence of **Air Traffic Control Towers (ATCT or Tower)**, early controllers used flags and hand held colored lights to signal landing and departure instructions to pilots. In 1930, the first airport to have a radio-equipped control tower was built in Cleveland. The Towers are always located at airports wherein the landing, departing and overflight traffic has grown to the extent that accidents are likely without someone on the ground keeping an eye on the sky. Smaller uncontrolled airports rely on pilots to tune to a common radio frequency (UNICOM) and announce their intentions. Busier airports may also have an Approach/Departure Control co-located with the Tower. These structures "own" the airspace immediately above and surrounding the airport.

A Tower's primary responsibilities revolve around a specific airport, they "own" the surface or movement areas including runways, taxiways, ramps, aprons, and the airspace within 5 miles laterally and about a thousand to two thousand feet vertically. (altitude varies) They are the most publically visible ATC presence since the building in which controllers work from must be tall enough to allow them to see all parts of the airport surface. The positions being worked are:

- **Clearance Delivery** – Pilots call here before they taxi to request a Clearance. In a towered environment, this consists of the pilot's instructions of what route he is to fly after he departs the ground. In some facilities the Clearance Delivery specialist is also handling Flight Data – monitoring the computer and phones for information updates. They may also be recording the ATIS weather and airport information broadcast.

- **Ground Control** - Once the aircraft is revved up and ready to move out of its parking spot, the ground controller directs them to the end of the active runway. The ground controller is also in contact with any ground service vehicles that happen to be in the movement areas such as fuel trucks, airport security, and baggage trains. They must also receive "clearance" to move between points.

- **Local Control** – This is the person pilots call "**tower**". The Local Controller is the one who ensures the runways and the airspace are "clear" of other traffic and then relays instructions for an aircraft to taxi into position on the runway, or cross a runway, and clears them for take off.

- **Coordinator** – The Coordinator sits next to the Local Controller, he acts as a second set of eyes during busy periods and takes the coordination calls coming in from Center, or Approach.

- **Approach Control** – The Approach and/or Departure controller monitors the airspace above and surrounding a specific airport. Originally these facilities were all co-located with the tower and the controllers would rotate between tower duties and approach duties. In today's world Approach facilities can be totally separated physically from the airport they serve, and in cases where there are several airports relatively close together, one specialist may be overseeing traffic at all of them.

  Their function is to separate and align air traffic coming and going within the confines of their airspace. They use radar to identify targets, their altitudes and their direction of travel.

Most Approach facilities contain more than one radar position, or **Sector.** One may only monitor aircraft arriving and departing to the east, with other sectors watching each of the other directions. They work closely together to feed all the aircraft into a line.

Since their radar is one site and focused on a smaller area, it is more

24

precise than that used by Center – so their standards of separation are closer.

Each sector may have one controller in direct communication with the pilots and an assistant who is coordinating clearances and handoffs with all the other ATC sectors both within the approach and with the associated Centers and Flight Service.

The **flight data** position handles incoming and outgoing computer data from other air traffic facilities and from the national flow control network.

Of course there are supervisors on duty overseeing the operation and making sure the controllers are relieved for breaks as needed.

Air Route Traffic Control Centers

The ARTCC's or "Centers" cover huge areas, usually several states wide. These huge facilities have 40 or 50 radar scopes and employ about 300 controllers plus support staff. Their airspace is divided both geographically and into high altitude and low altitude sectors.

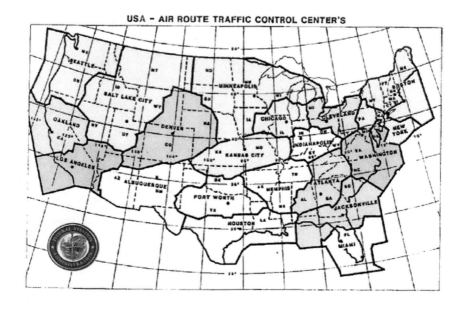

USA – AIR ROUTE TRAFFIC CONTROL CENTER'S

Have you looked on aviation charts and noticed that the Center boundaries are oddly shaped? That's partially because they were not all created at once. A consortium of commercial airlines and airport operators established the first three Centers, Cleveland, Chicago and Newark, during late 1935 through June 1936. The Bureau of Air Commerce, within the Department of Commerce (DOC), took over their operation when it assumed responsibility for what was eventually known as "air traffic control" or ATC in July of 1936. As air traffic density moved west, new Centers were created to manage the flows.

Each time, the protected airspace was built primarily around the areas containing a dense population of aircraft. As a result you had three Centers in the northeast, followed by a couple in Georgia and Florida, followed by California. Over time they decided to "fill in" the areas so that all airspace over the continental United States was assigned to a control facility.

Early enroute controllers tracked aircraft positions on maps and blackboards using little wedge-shaped weights called "shrimp boats." There was no direct communication capability between controllers and aircraft at the time, so they used telephones to stay in touch with airline dispatchers, airway radio operators, and airport traffic controllers, who also fed information to the enroute controllers and relayed their instructions to pilots.

Today each Center handles several states traffic, and advances in technology have increased the ability of the Controllers to more accurately determine the placement of aircraft in their airspace. The latest merging of radar, satellite and computer functions used by the Centers is known as the En Route Automation Modernization (ERAM) computer. The accuracy of this system allows closer, more accurate placement of aircraft in our increasingly crowded airspace.

The ARTCC sectors are separated both geographically and by altitude. In the busiest areas you may have three layers. The lowest will be from the surface to at least 18,000 feet – the bottom of the Positive Control area. In that area controllers will work a mix of VFR and IFR traffic, but above 18,000 feet all aircraft must be IFR.

The next sector may overlay the first geographically, but the controller is only working traffic between 18,000 feet and 30,000 feet (or FL180 to FL300). The third sector will work the aircraft above 30,000 through 60,000 feet. Above 60,000 feet (or flight level 600) traffic is mostly military, experimental, or rocketry. Air Carriers normally have the best fuel consumption between 28,000 and 45,000.

The stratification helps controllers work departing/landing aircraft up and down through the flight levels to their requested altitudes.

Sectors are adjusted according to the traffic they serve. In the west, Albuquerque Center has one sector wherein the controller works aircraft from the surface to 60,000. Restricted airspace precludes most air carrier traffic, but military aircraft are practicing maneuvers that may require them to "go vertical" right after takeoff.

Like the Approach Controls, each sector has at least two controllers during daylight hours – one talking to the pilots and giving them the clearance instructions while the other is working the computer and taking calls from other sectors and facilities. Really busy sectors and times of day may necessitate a third controller standing behind the other two providing support

Besides general administration, ARTCC support staff includes a military liason, and a National Weather Service group whose job it is to focus on how weather will affect the traffic in that Center's airspace and issue appropriate alerts. The Centers have personnel who work with the national Air Traffic

Flow Management team. These specialists send instructions out to the sectors when they need specific aircraft slowed, turned or even re-routed. This happens when too many aircraft are inbound to a specific location, when weather or something unexpected closes an airport or when there is an incident involving national security.

Another group of specialists are coordinating **flight data** between ATC facilities and notifying the sectors whenever a Temporary Flight Restriction, or Notice to Airmen affecting them is issued.

Flight Service Stations

Flight Service was the first branch of ATC, it evolved from the army air corps flight planners and trackers developed in World War I. The excitement and innovation of aircraft allowed people access to the skies, and opened up a hunger for a new experience...and a need for support personnel on the ground.

When aviation was first developed there were no airports – aircraft landed or took off from a field or a beach – anyplace relatively flat and open. The first routes with set landing zones were developed by the post office. The specialists who were posted in these often remote spots had a very short range radio they were expected to maintain. They had timetables for when the Air Mail planes should arrive. As they came within radio range the pilot would call the specialists to get information on weather and wind directions. If it was raining or night time the specialist would light a fire on oil soaked wood in a metal wheelbarrow to mark the ends of the landing area. After the aircraft landed they'd help unload or load the aircraft and make sure the pilot had help with anything he needed.

The most important aspect of flight service was the responsibility to keep track of overdue aircraft. A specific series of steps was developed to implement search and rescue when aircraft did not arrive on time that is still in use today.

That legacy of service to the aviation community carried Flight Service personnel through the next hundred years. Over time they no longer had to repair their own equipment or light up the runways at night, but they have always been the facility pilots can go to for assistance with a variety of services.

Today's automated **Flight Service Station (AFSS)** handles a diversity of pilot needs. The physical structure can be located at an airport, but modern technology has removed that requirement since everything the AFSS does is by phone or radio. Flight Service briefs pilots on preflight conditions including weather, hazardous conditions and anything significant they may encounter on their flight. They take flight plans and they monitor the progress of VFR aircraft (aircraft flying uncontrolled below 18,000 feet). They still initiate search and rescue should a VFR aircraft become overdue, act as an interface with both the other branches of ATC and related government agencies, such as Customs, Homeland Security, and the military.

Other duties of Flight Service include updating pilots on weather enroute; inputting weather and PIREP data, and inputting Notices to Airmen (NOTAMs) into the national data base.

Chapter 4

The Future of ATC

We live in exciting times right now because the FAA is in the process of revising the entire ATC system. Rampant growth and the creation of new facilities was the hallmark of the first 50 years of ATC. As aviation caught the imagination and passion of individual pilots and commercial applications grew, facilities were built and procedures were devised and implemented to increase safety and efficiency. At one time there were over 400 Flight Service Stations located mostly at small to medium airports not boasting towers. Over time their responsibilities evolved from simply taking weather observations, and monitoring flight activities at a single airport to taking radio calls and giving phone briefings over multi-state areas.

With advances in technology Air Route Traffic Control Centers could "see" aircraft positions in relation to each other and to the terrain on a mapped radar screen. Towers began by using flag signals to aircraft, then hand held spotlights color coded to give landing clearances. Radar and better radios stimulated the development of Approach and Departure control facilities.

Computer and technology leaps allowed the FAA to reduce costs by consolidating the Flight Service Stations beginning in the late 1980's. By 2000 there were approximately one per state left with Texas and California having a couple extra. Alaska remained unchanged.

In the late 1990's congress began looking for ways to privatize services that had been traditionally run by the federal government, and continue to reduce costs.

In 2005 the FAA Administrational offices were redistributed along regional lines. Many smaller Towers were contracted to being administered by private companies but subject to FAA oversight. Also in 2005 Flight Service was turned over to Lockheed Martin to manage. The controller workforce were all government employees on October 3rd, and Lockheed Martin employees on October 4th. Within the next 5 years Flight Service was further consolidated into three main Hub facilities with two small satellite facilities. In 2016 Lockheed Martin turned over the Flight Service administration contract to Leidos.

Over the next twenty years you will see more Approach/Departure controls being completely separated from the airports they serve and many will be housed with the Centers. The Center boundaries will be changing as well. By requiring any aircraft that fly within positive control airspace to install ADS-B systems, the ability for Air Traffic to always be able to find aircraft that go missing rises dramatically. This will greatly enhance ATC's ability to pinpoint the location of aircraft who have crashed or had to land in mountainous terrain, or lakes.

One new system being implemented is the Next Generation Air Transport System, (NexGen) which will primarily affect the airlines and executive aircraft, and dramatically change ATC as we know it. For more information go to www.jpdo.aero, or www.faa.gov.

Trust

I am sometimes humbled by the great, enormous amount of trust that pilots place in the US Air Traffic Control system, and the controllers who serve them. I remember one time, after I had become a Flight Watch Specialist at Albuquerque AFSS I spoke to a pilot who was traveling through the Texas panhandle. He had gotten a briefing 3 hours earlier before the radars even showed a glimpse of the afternoon's thunderstorms. Suddenly he found himself surrounded by rapidly growing cells, in front and behind.

He called Flight Watch rather than Center because he knew my weather radar could show storms better than the ATC radars the Centers use. He gave me his radial/DME off of the Dalhart VORTAC.

I looked at the growth pattern and movement of the cells. I knew if he kept on his present course to the southeast he would run into a big patch that had just begun some rapid upward development. He gave me his airspeed and heading. Because he was VFR I could not order him to do anything, but I did suggest that, maintaining VFR, he turn to a heading of 240 degrees and fly for ten minutes, then turn to 180 degrees for 5 minutes, then back to 240 to skinny out of the area.

It worked. He landed at Childress to fuel and re-think his flight to San Antonio.

This is the kind of thing that can only happen when there is trust between the pilots and the controllers, and it is the kind of thing that we can go home at the end of the day and truly feel good about.

Chapter 5

Careers in Air Traffic Control

Though this book is designed primarily as a tool for pilots to understand their relationship to ATC, whenever I lecture on the topic there are always questions on how to become an Air Traffic Controller.

The rules are changing. To enter the Tower or Center options you can still, as of the printing of this book, meet the following qualifications: You must have at least 3 years of progressively responsible full time work experience or a bachelor's degree, and be under the age of 31. You must be a U.S. Citizen and be able to speak English clearly.

Then you must take the ATC exam, which is only scheduled a few times a year by the US Office of Personnel Management. Although the government in general considers 70% to generally be a passing grade, you will not be called for the next step unless you score 90% or over.

If you do score 90% or over, the FAA may call you for an interview. They will also require a medical exam by an authorized FAA doctor, a psychiatric exam, a drug test and a security/background check. The medical exam has stringent vision and hearing tests.

Once you pass all of those, your name is put on a list. When a position becomes open in one of the ATC options you have requested consideration for, in a part of the country you have already stated you would be willing to work, they will call and ask you to accept that position. Your odds are better if you pre-designate that you will work in any option, anywhere in the country. Once you have achieved full performance level (FPL), you can bid to move to other facilities.

If you are called for a job, and decline, your name may be moved to the bottom of the list. For many years this was the only way to get into ATC. At the dawn of the 21st century, the FAA broadened your options. They instituted the Air Traffic Collegiate Training Initiative (AT-CTI). There are designated colleges around the US offering degree programs in aviation and air traffic. Students graduating from these programs may be recommended by the college to the FAA as Air Traffic Candidates. As openings become available, the candidates are offered an opportunity to go to the academy.

One thing to keep in mind is that retirement from this job is currently mandatory at age 56. There is compelling medical evidence that physical deterioration begins around that age, and the job requires good eyesight, hearing, decision making capabilities and other baseline physical competency. Many controllers opt to transfer into administrative jobs as they reach their early 50's, which allows them to continue working.

If you want more information you can check out the FAA website at www.faa.gov/jobs. The website also contains the list of the FAA's approved colleges for Air Traffic degrees.

When Flight Service was privatized, the corporation instituted their own hiring program which requires a college degree in aviation. Persons who graduate from the approved colleges could apply directly to LMCO whenever the company posts job availability. This procedure is not expected to change when LMCO hands off the Flight Service Contract during their merger with Leidos. All Flight Service Specialists must still pass the FAA's medical, security and psychiatric requirements, but at this time are not subject to mandatory retirement.

A last note, before applying for a job in Air Traffic, keep in mind that there is a significant amount of stress associated with this job. Statistically, only doctors and pilots have a higher divorce rate. Stress levels are higher at facilities which handle higher levels of traffic. As the Controller's paycheck is directly linked with what level of facility he/she works for, at some time you may have to decide how greedy you are versus how much you want to preserve your sanity.

The Psychology of ATC
(Letter from a reader of the Atlantic Flyer)

Dear Rose Marie

I recently discovered that I have a significant interest in a career in Air Traffic Control. However, the dilemma for me is that it's not something that's very well publicized. I find it hard to tell what personality traits would make for a good ATC.

I wouldn't want to spend the time and money getting an associate's degree from the local community college and then apply to the FAA only to find out I'm a horrible match for the job. If you could provide any insight to what it's really like, would be good and what traits could be detrimental, I'd certainly appreciate it. Thank you very much for your time.
Regards,
Justin

Dear Justin

Your request involves divining interesting personal information about the types of people that make good controllers. The answer is both simple and complex. In 1983 when I started with Air Traffic, the Civil Aeronautical Medical Institute (CAMI) was giving the trainees ongoing tests to try to determine who would be able to make it through the training and become a controller and who would not.

As we went through the academy, every single test we took had "CAMI" questions woven into the test. These questions had no real correct answer and were not counted in the grades, but you never knew which ones they were because they pertained to the material.

I do not know if CAMI ever discovered their "perfect" profile for a successful controller or not. I can tell you that whether someone made it through the training or not, there did not seem to be any rhyme or reason personality wise. I have worked with some people who were highly intelligent, and some who seemed like backwoods hicks, some with Doctorates and some who just skimmed through school and some average people who worked in a totally unrelated field before taking the ATC exam. (Like me). The only thing the successful people had in common was that they could "see" traffic, apply the rules correctly, and make decisions and follow through on them efficiently. Most of them are also the types that you want around in an emergency.

The training requires you to learn how to be totally confident in yourself. I walked in the door with no knowledge of ATC at all. I made it through the academy and spent the next two years training at Albuquerque Air Route Traffic Control Center. After the academic portion, you spend hours every day with someone sitting behind you with a clipboard writing down every misspoken word and notating any procedural errors. If you cannot take criticism - this will drive you nuts. As you master each sector you "check out" on the sector and your training on other sectors is interspersed with working the positions you are now qualified on to work alone.

What's the difference between options? ARTCC's are big dark rooms full of radar scopes and computers. Each ARTCC controls a large portion of airspace. Albuquerque ARTCC controls the area from west Texas almost to the California border and from Mexico to Colorado/Utah. The airspace is divided into specialties (north, Southwest, Southeast, East, etc). The specialties are divided into sectors - high altitude and low altitude covering a specific portion of the area. As a trainee you are assigned to a specialty. ARTCC controllers along with the highest level tower/approach controllers make the most money in ATC and have the highest stress option - both because it is the most difficult to check out in and because the traffic is usually fairly dense. The ARTCC's in Albuquerque, Denver, and Salt Lake have the lowest traffic count/less stress. East and west coast are highest traffic count/stress. If you are an adrenaline junkie who thrives on challenges - this is where you want to be.

Towers have a lot of various levels, and if I'd known what I know now when I started, I probably would have held out for one. Usually you start in a lower level to get your ticket, then if you want to move or earn a higher paycheck you bid on towers with higher levels of traffic. The only bad part is that every time you change facilities, you also go through training again, but the assumption is that if you have become a full performance level controller (FPL) at a lower level facility, you have the basic skills needed to learn a new area. Many lower traffic level towers are now privatized, so the FAA will start trainees in mid-level towers.

Many of the older flight service (FSS) people, like myself, worked in other facilities first and then moved laterally. Flight Service does not make the salary that the ARTCC's and some towers do, but it is more friendly and in my opinion requires someone more academically inclined than the others. FSS duties require a greater knowledge base - all of us have to be certified as pilot weather briefers by the National Weather Service. We talk to pilots both on the ground prior to their flights as well as in the air. We are the ones who begin search and rescue for pilots who do not show up at their destinations.

ARTCC people are disembodied voices that give commands to pilots and never really meet or interact with them. Towers are likewise in the busier environments, though some smaller towers have people who develop relationships with their aviation community. Flight Service people are focused on the needs of individual pilots - and frequently develop a camaraderie with them.

The requirements to get into any of the ATC fields have changed a lot since I hired on, but once in the door the training requirements are about the same. It is much easier to check out in FSS and Tower then in an ARTCC, but the end reward in ARTCC is a higher paycheck than the others. So part of choosing which direction to go revolves around how much you see yourself earning.

When you are first hired on you are required to pass an interview, a psychological test, a physical, and a security check. At this time there is also an age requirement for ARTCC and Tower work - you cannot be any older than 31. FSS has no age restrictions.

You can visit the various ATC facilities by calling one and making an appointment for a tour. Tell whoever answers the phone that you are thinking of a career. When you call an ARTCC ask for the Human Relations person - who will also have the latest info on how to get into the job.

One more thing to know, all air traffic branches are required to work under a Union. ARTCC and Federal Towers are represented by the National Air Traffic Control Association or NATCA. www.NATCA.org. Flight Service is under the International Association of Machinists (IAM) http://www.goiam.org/afss.

Whether you are forced to actually pay union dues or not depends on what state you live in. Regardless, you have no vote if you are not a member and must work by their rules. There are pluses and minuses to unions - and everyone is passionate about them - for or against.

One final note, this is not a job where things once you've gotten your certification the learning stops. In addition to continuous refresher training, the rapid development of new technologies requires procedures to be updated. The installation of new equipment requires everyone in air traffic to bring an open minded attitude to change.

These are all personal observations, but I hope they give you some insights

Rose Marie

All in a Day's Work

For about two hours every morning, traffic runs high at the Centers. There is a constant low hum of voices giving clearances and coordinating actions with surrounding Sectors. Toward the end of this time period one morning, a controller suddenly rolled backwards away from the radar scope and quoting the Pointer Sisters song yelled at the top of his lungs, "I'M ABOUT TO LOSE CONTROL AND I THINK I LIKE IT!!!"

The impromptu joke broke the tension of the morning rush as everyone laughed then turned back to their radar scopes.

To my knowledge, there has never been a TV sitcom about air traffic control. The media has regularly made fun of cops, doctors, swat teams, and the military, but the only movie I've seen that truly poked fun specifically at controllers was "Pushing Tin". I gotta admit, the guy that wrote that one has spent real, quality time with Air Traffic Controllers who work in a high traffic environment – about half of the ones I know have at least a smidgen of that "I am always right" competitive attitude.

The moviemaker did do something else well that most people don't truly understand. There are several sequences where the camera is "looking" into the radar screen, and suddenly you "see" the way the aircraft are moving in a three dimensional way.

I have known some controllers that you would say are really intelligent, complete with PH.D.'s and some that were the dumbest rednecks you have ever seen. Some of them are ex-military, and some are musicians, cowboys, and beekeepers. Some of them are pilots who love not only what they do, but everything else related to flying.

The common denominator between all of them is the ability to "see" traffic, to communicate effectively with pilots, and to know absolutely that the instructions that they are giving the pilot will guide them safely to their destinations.

Chapter 6

Check out the FAA Website

For anyone who is curious about aviation, the FAA website, www.faa.gov, has a plethora of useful information. You can look up TFR's, Airport NOTAMs, who an aircraft is registered to, the history of the FAA, and how to get a job in Air Traffic Control.

In the modern world of computer access, many pilots like to self-brief. Websites for weather abound these days, but where is the best place to look for NOTAMs and airport delays? The FAA website home page on the top right says AIRPORT DELAYS. The graphic shows only the major airports across the country. Green means no delay, yellow has some delays and a number to indicate how long, and red means ground stop. You may not be going into the larger airports, but if you are going to a smaller one close by, you might want to look hard at the expected weather in the area, or if there are other reasons for the delays. If the large airports are experiencing major delays, surrounding airports may get busier as aircraft are diverted.

A major concern are Temporary Flight Restrictions, or TFR's. Although TFR's can be issued for anything that constitutes a hazard to flight (forest fires, gas pipe blowouts etc...) most pilots are on the lookout for the VIP TFR. Back to the home page – then halfway down the page on the right under Regulations and Guidelines you will find TEMPORARY FLIGHT

43

RESTRICTIONS.   A list is provided, but what is most helpful is to click on the bar above where it says TFR MAP. A graphic of the U.S. will appear with red circles, squares or other odd markings. If one seems close to your route, click on it to enlarge the area – keep clicking until it shows up as an overlay on a VFR Sectional Chart to see exactly where it is, read the text of that TFR to understand altitudes and specific location data.

The VIP TFRs can still be a bit tricky as they have multiple parts and different rules at different times. If you look at it and cannot determine whether your airport will be affected, call Flight Service – they keep lists of which airports are being affected by the TFRs. Do not take the times listed in the TFR as gospel. Those are the target times, but delays have been known to happen. The TFR may state from 1200z to 1900z, but if the aircraft containing the exalted personage the TFR was created for has not left the ground yet, the TFR is still in effect until it has. Flight Service will have the latest information as to whether the TFR is still in effect.

Another part of the FAA website that is useful for each flight under the Regulations and Policies tab is Notices to Airmen (NOTAMS) – this is in the left sidebar. Clicking it brings you to the FAA's Pilot Web page. You can look up specific locations, or do a flight path search. The default for the flight path search is 25 NM either side of a direct route between locations. This works pretty well for flights on the eastern third of the country, but out west you might want to increase that buffer a bit.   One warning, increasing the buffer means it takes the site longer to bring up your data. Be patient.

You need to specify what you want the computer to bring up – just the NOTAMs at your departure and destination? All the airports and navaids enroute? How about the FDC and ARTCC Notams? A lot of pilots skip the latter, but what if the ARTCC NOTAM states that GPS could be unreliable or unavailable within a 400NMR of a given point?

Knowing one of those NOTAMs was in effect for southern New Mexico, I pulled out a hand held GPS while standing on a point west of Roswell. The GPS showed me to be 30 miles south of the Mexican border!

The FAA website contains other information and statistics of interest to the General Aviation pilot. Under Aviation Forecasts you will not find weather – you will find the FAA's guesses as to the growth patterns of aviation over the next 30 years. You can get insights into the direction the FAA wants to go by clicking on the Plans and Priorities tab, and check out what NextGen is and how it will affect ATC as all the components come online.

Say there is a really nice looking Skyhawk sitting next to yours on the ramp. You notice an interesting modification and want to find the owner so you can ask him about it. On the www.faa.gov home page on the left is the category AIRCRAFT. Under the subcategory AIRCRAFT CERTIFICATION you can type in the tail number, and it will show you who owns the aircraft.

People who are buying drones are directed to the FAA.gov website to research the rules for flying them. The FAA has three categories: Public (governmental), Civil (Commercial) and Hobby. Most of the Public and Civil drone operators are required to obtain waivers and file NOTAMs for their flights. Hobby drones usually do not – as long as they meet the specifications shown on the FAA website.

Thinking about going into space? The FAA issues a commercial space transportation license. If you want to put a runway out on the back 40, do you have to have airport certification? What is the difference between an experimental aircraft and a sport aircraft? Why do they have different regulations? It's all there…www.faa.gov.

The first Air Mail Radio Station or AMRS was commissioned in 1920 in Bellefont, PA. The AMRS's were the forerunners of the modern Flight Service Stations.

Chapter 7

The History of Flight Service

Did you know that Flight Service was originally a division of the Post Office? In combination with the Army, the Post Office developed Air Mail Routes along the east coast. Then in 1918, the military transferred operations to the Post Office and by 1920 a transcontinental route was established with 17 Air Mail Radio Stations (AMRS) in activation

Then, as now, the specialists at the AMRS's gathered and disseminated weather data, but their duties also included maintaining equipment, servicing the aircraft and unloading mail. As many of them were former maritime radio operators, they were expected to maintain their own equipment.

The Air Commerce Act of 1926 transferred the budding airway systems initially to the control of the Bureau of Lighthouses under the Department of Commerce. But the need for a separate administration was recognized and so the Airways Division was created in 1927. Once of their first acts was to rename their 45 facilities "Airways Radio Stations" or ARS.

This was an exciting time in aviation as the "rules" of the air were being developed, airways were created and methods of communication were invented. Messages between the ARS's were sent by teletype starting in

1928, and many of the Q codes still recognized in Flight Service began as short cuts in order to enhance quick communication. Today we still refer to the first stage of Search and Rescue as a QALQ.

Morse Code was the primary method of communication prior to the development of voice transmission. VORTAC's today still broadcast in that manner. Fortunately for us all, voice communication was recognized early on as the most efficient and effective way to insure safety, and its development was made a top priority.

The Civil Aeronautics Authority (CAA) was created in 1938, and the ARS became the Airway Communication Station or ACS. Skilled electronic technicians were introduced to the system to maintain the equipment, allowing the specialists more time to serve their primary function of assisting the pilots.

During World War II, the military utilized the ACSs heavily, and women began "manning" the facilities as the men went off to war. After the war, aviation experienced tremendous growth as air carriers and private pilots surged into the sky.

1958 saw the creation of the Federal Aviation Agency, and the ACS's finally became what we know today as Flight Service Stations (FSS).

The FSS specialist's duties by this time were more focused on the needs of the flying public. A Search and Rescue system had been developed and communication was vastly improved. Training and Certification from the National Weather Service enhanced the specialist's abilities to provide tailored and more complete information to the pilots.

The 50's also had some nasty aviation accidents that highlighted a need for better radio communications and navigational facilities. This spurred the government to focus on the needs of the Tower's and Centers, and FSS's importance faded somewhat in the grand scheme of things. While the others received the latest in computers, Flight Service continued to trudge along with teletype.

The Department of Transportation took over the Federal Aviation Administration in 1967, and recognition of the importance of real time weather information during flights became apparent. This led to what we now know as Flight Watch or Enroute Flight Advisory Service (EFAS) in 1972.

About 400 FSS;s were in operation by the early 1970's, but advances in technology and the implementation of new computer systems encouraged the FAA to consolidate these facilities into 61 Automated Flight Services from 1984 to 1997. Alaska was the only state to retain just over a dozen of the smaller 1 and 2 man stations.

Consolidation of the smaller facilities into the larger Hubs began the dissolution of a relationship between flight service personnel and the pilots they served. When the services were located on the fields the pilots would come into the building and have a cup of coffee while being briefed. Flight Service people frequently socialized with the pilots and knew their families. If an aircraft went missing, it would affect them personally.

Three different computer systems were installed in these facilities, which created some interface problems, and the FAA was in the process of changing all of them over to an advanced graphics and data system called OASIS when the US government decided that Flight Service could and should be administrated through contracts with a corporation rather than directly by the federal government.

A study to privatize Flight Service began in 2001, and by 2003 we knew that changes would happen. In March of 2005 it was announced that Lockheed Martin (LM) would be awarded the contract, and the official change of command for those stations in the lower 48 states plus Hawaii occurred in October of that year.

Poster distributed by the FAA to celebrate
Flight Service History the year that the
Flight Service Division was privatized.

As of the first quarter of 2007, Lockheed's FS21 computer came online, simultaneously the number of physical Flight Service Stations was reduced to today's total of 18. The three main Hubs are in Washington DC, Prescott, and Fort Worth. These are the administrative centers for the three regions: Eastern, Central and Western. Since 2013 Flight Service has the three Hubs and two smaller briefing only facilities.

The FS21 computer system had a rocky beginning, but improvements are implemented every two weeks or so. Whereas the old computer systems were set up locally and only shared information that was "emailed" between facilities, the main advantage of the FS21 rests primarily in its ability to interface nationally. Specialists in Maine have access to all the data input by Briefers in California.

As part of its overall plan, Lockheed implemented a website component that pilots can access remotely. It contains all the weather data available to Flight Service and provides an entry point for flight plan information. In 2016 Flight Service was put under the control of the Leidos Corporation.

For more information about FS-21 and Flight Service Strategies visit their website at www.afss.com.

The goals and services provided have changed over time, but the main thrust of Flight Service is to provide the pilot with all the information needed to have a safe, enjoyable flight, knowing that if he needs help, there is a place he can call.

Information needed for a Standard Weather Briefing

VFR or IFR
Aircraft Identification
Type of Aircraft
Type of transponder equipment
Departure Point
Estimated Time of Departure
Altitude
Route of Flight
Destination
Estimated Time Enroute

Chapter 8

Painless Pilot Weather Briefing
(Or how to Help Flight Service Brief You)

In air traffic it is a joke that an Air Traffic Controller tells pilots where to go. But a Flight Service Specialist tells pilots where NOT to go, and his method of doing that is by using a standard weather briefing format.

You have no idea how nice it is to have a pilot call and rattle off (slowly) something like this:

"Hi, I am VFR experimental N5LP going from Albuquerque at 1430 zulu at one-two-thousand via Gallup to Flagstaff with two hours and 15 minutes enroute."

That is BEAUTIFUL, in 15 seconds the pilot has given me everything needed for a standard briefing. The data that the computer spits out is based on that information. Most of the time the pilot will state a few items, and then the specialist has to ask for the rest – and sometimes pilots will say "I don't want a flight plan, just a weather briefing." At that point most specialists usually stop and explain a flight plan is not being filed, but much of the same information is needed to bring up the briefing data. Here is what Flight Service briefers need before they can begin the briefing and why.

VFR or IFR This tells a briefer whether or not you, as the pilot, have the training and instrumentation to fly through clouds. The specialist cannot make a judgment as to whether a pilot SHOULD go IFR or VFR, it is not their job to determine a pilot's abilities. Briefers need to know what you, the pilot, want to do, and whether or not I need to let you know that VFR is not recommended due to inclement weather or if the briefing needs to include two pages worth of arrival and departure NAVAID NOTAMS because you are flying IFR.

Aircraft ID or Call Sign All briefs, radio calls, and other data are recorded by the aircraft's call sign – not the pilot's name. The computer requires this entry to get to the briefing data. Also, if someone is overdue and a panicked relative calls flight service, be sure they know the aircraft ID.

If you know that you are going to be renting an aircraft, but you do not have a tail number yet, then we can list it as NOACID and put the pilot's name in remarks, but if you want to make sure your bases are covered, try to have it available.

Type Aircraft Let's face it, a small aircraft flying low and slow needs different information than a Learjet. Skyhawks do not need jet stream information, and a Learjet could care less about cloud bases enroute.

This section has elicited a lot of confusion over the past few years. Many pilots do not recall that there was a widespread re-identification of aircraft types about 10 years ago. It was one of those FAA documents that went out to everyone that says that after 30 years of a Cherokee being a PA28, all of a sudden it is designated as a P28A.

It did not really matter much to the private pilot because he could still call his flight plan over to FSS and the old computers would take PA28 as usual.

However, the new FS21 computers "know" that there is no longer a PA28 or a HS25 or a T-45 type of aircraft – so they will not accept the flight plan until the correct aircraft type designator is used. If you have any questions as to what your identifier is, Flight Service can help you look it up.

ATC computers only have 4 spaces in the Aircraft type section of the flight plan form. I know you love your airplane, but if you tell me you have a Turbo C210 Retractable with all kinds of fancy modifications…..well, that's nice……all I have room for on the form is C210.

Departure Point-Route-Destination   Ok, it seems obvious, but I cannot tell you how many times a pilot wants to go from Albuquerque to Phoenix, but neglects to tell the briefer that they are doing it by flying the valleys a hundred miles south of a direct course to avoid high mountains, or that he is really departing Albuquerque's Double Eagle Airport 15 miles west of the main Albuquerque Airport going to Chandler Municipal in the Phoenix area.

Unless the right data is given the first time, the specialist is not able to get the specific weather and NOTAM information for your airport, and if a direct route is assumed, then you would not be briefed about a Temporary Flight Restriction over the valley area for forest fires.

Be sure you know the identifiers for your route of flight. You'll be on the phone longer if the briefer has to look them up for you. And even if you are VFR, please list your route according to aviation NAVAIDS or airports – the computer does not recognize lakes and highways. If you file a flight plan later you can add lakes, highways and/or towns in remarks.

Altitude   Most aviation professionals are good at guessing at what altitudes various aircraft can fly, but if you want the wind forecasts specify an altitude. Also, it's OK to ask for winds at several altitudes and the briefer's opinion as to which altitude would be best.

What cracks me and most of the people I work with up, is when the pilots "blame" us for a headwind and thank us for a tailwind!

Departure Time   PLEASE, PLEASE, PLEASE learn to convert to ZULU! Each of us briefs pilots in time zones across the country. If someone in Hobokan, Indiana calls up and says he is departing at 5pm local time – we may end up in a 5 minute conversation as to what that is in Greenwich Mean Time (ZULU). (Did you know that until recently Indiana had three different time zones?)

If you just cannot get the conversion mentally, a cheat to this is to simply say you are leaving in 30 minutes...or 5 hours. It's easy to add this to the current Zulu time.

If you choose to file a flight plan later, that it stays in the computer of the agency that you filed it with until an hour prior to the proposal time, then it is transmitted to whatever AFSS or Center will be activating it. So if you call for departure more than an hour prior to the time your flight is proposed for, and you filed with DUATS, a baseops, or some other entity, the Tower (if IFR) or Radio (VFR), may not have received it yet. Also, the flight plan stays active on Tower and Radio proposed list for two hours past the proposal time before dropping out.

Time Enroute   This last item allows us to calculate the time period for which we need to scan weather and NOTAMs.

The computer system is designed to route your call to the place you request first, but if all the Briefers for that location are busy, rather than keep you on hold it will look for someone who normally Briefs in the next adjacent area. However, if there is specific information about the airport or terrain you are flying into, you may want to ask the computer to route you to a briefer that handles your destination airport. Any Flight Service can file flight plans from anywhere in the country, but if you want to know specific data about flying restrictions around the Grand Canyon, you might want to ask for Arizona.

Keep in mind that because weather is always updated between the hour and 5 minutes past the hour, the best time to call for a briefing will always be 10 to 20 minutes after the hour.

The worst time is between 5 minutes till and 5 minutes after the hour. In most flight service stations, specialists rotate from the Pre-flight briefing position, through Flight Data, Radio, and other specialized positions every few hours, to keep from getting stale, and this dance starts at 5 minutes till the hour. For about 10 minutes, the specialists are giving and receiving our transfer of position briefings and changing the computer settings. As a result, this is when you will run the highest chance of being on hold.

Following the above format as you request a briefing is easiest for the briefer because she or he is tabbing between fields in the computer as you speak – if you give us the above data out of order, we may end up asking you to repeat information several times as we jump around on the page, wasting a lot of your precious time!

Kittyhawk

Chapter 9

Do You Want "Any Briefer"?

I read in AOPA's magazine that the fastest way for pilots to get through to a weather briefer is to call the 1-800-WXBRIEF number and say "Any Briefer". Well, they are right, this is the way to get someone fast, but is this what you really want? When you say "Any Briefer" the phone tree will send your call to the first available specialist — without regard to where you are calling from, or what you want to know.

There are times when this is just fine. For instance, if all you want to do is file a flight plan, "Any Briefer" will do. Other times when "Any Briefer" is appropriate include canceling a VFR flight plan, filing a pilot report, or asking general ATC questions. Just keep in mind that since you could be talking to someone not familiar with your area, you should have all the identifiers to fixes along your route handy.

If what you want is a preflight briefing, especially low altitude, you probably will want to talk to a Briefer who is familiar with your area within a few hundred miles. They will more than likely know things about the terrain, the airports, and the weather patterns that someone from far away will not.

Briefers have noted that pilots calling in using the "Any Briefer" are frustrated when the person they are speaking to is unfamiliar with aviation designators enroute, forcing the pilot to spell them all phonetically.

The Flight Service phone tree is set up so that if you call and ask for East Texas, and it happens that all the Briefers assigned to East Texas are busy, within a few seconds the system starts looking for an available Briefer in the surrounding areas. It starts close in to where you are and circles outbound until it finds someone to take your call.

This accomplishes two things: it reduces your hold time, and it attempts to get your call to someone familiar with the area you want information for. This system has significantly reduced hold times nationwide.

If you absolutely have to speak to someone qualified in a specific location, whoever answers your call can put your call back into the queue for that area. In this case your call will stay in the queue until someone from that facility is available, which may involve holding for a few minutes.

Another thing to keep in mind is that the system allows you flexibility when you need some information from some other place. For example, if you are in Arkansas and you want to take your kids to the Grand Canyon. While making your plans you can call the 1-800-WX BRIEF phone number and ask for Arizona. The specialists in Prescott can let you know what procedures you need to follow if you want to fly the Canyon.

Another example would be a pilot who primarily flies in the plains and wants to go to Eagle, Colorado – when calling for a briefing he should say "Colorado" instead of his home state. He should mention to the briefer that he is flying into the mountains for the first time and would not mind some advice on routes and the effects of mountains waves. In the winter Colorado has many ski area airports with STMP's, or Special Traffic Management Procedures – you definitely want to know about them before you fly!

Pilots can ask for Illinois, Indiana, Michigan or Ohio to learn about flying the Great Lakes area. Have a question about the famous Santa Ana winds? Call California. This is a valuable tool for getting specific information well in advance of the actual flight.

The highest call volumes are between 6am and 10am in each time zone nationwide. Keeping this in mind, we suggest that if you do want pre-planning information give Flight Service a call later in the day as a courtesy to other pilots whose flights are imminent.

The phone system also separates Briefing functions from Clearance Delivery and NOTAM functions. IFR Clearance Delivery nationwide is 1-888-766-8267. When you call that number you will always get a specialist in the state you have specified, even if you have to hold for a few minutes until they are free. Briefers in other areas may not be able to access the correct Air Route Traffic Control Center, so using this phone number is essential. If you file Lifeguard on occasion, you can call flight service and ask for the phone number that is only given out for Lifeguard clearances.

By the same token if you are a westerner planning a flight to the D.C. area and are nervous about the SFRA and FRZ procedures, the call tree has a special phone number just for this information 866-225-7410

Another special phone number is only for helicopter operations over the Gulf of Mexico. Call 1-877-654-7449 if you are a helicopter pilot. The specialists who answer this line are familiar with the routings and squawk code requirements of flying over the Gulf.

Some pilots have problems with the voice recognition feature of the phone tree. In this case you can use the touch tone pad on your phone to request the state of your choice. Most of the states are simply the postal abbreviation – for example, Arizona is AZ or 29. A list of the codes is posted on the www.afss.com website under "Pilot tips".

The Flight Service phone tree allows you great flexibility when it comes to flight planning and briefs. Be sure you know what you want before you call and ask for "Any Briefer" and you will have a more pleasant briefing experience.

Chapter 10

Types of Weather Briefings

There are three types of briefings a pilot can call for: Standard, Abbreviated and Outlook.

The **Standard** weather briefing presents the range of information that the FAA has deemed necessary to 95% of flights in a specific format. First the *Adverse Conditions* tell you what weather related hazards to the flight exist, and any other item that may keep you from flying, such as Temporary Flight Restrictions or NOTAMS relating to runway and airport closures.

Then the *Synopsis* reveals what atmospheric conditions are creating the hazards. If you are flying using Visual Flight Rules (VFR) and the weather indicates that this type of flight is not possible, then this is usually where the Briefer will state "VFR not recommended."

After that you receive the *Current Conditions* along your route. This portion of the brief consists of a combination of the METARs (surface reports at stations connected to the National Weather Service system) as well as radar and satellite data as appropriate.

The next portion consists of information that has been given to the National Weather Service concerning flight conditions at your altitudes by other pilots. These *Pilot Reports* or PIREPS are kept in the computer for only one hour to insure that they are timely.

Now the brief moves into the areas of forecast. The *Enroute Forecast* put out by the National Weather Service, and the *Terminal Forecast* or TAF allows you to receive information for both specific stations and for the entire area your flight will transit. Then you are given the *forecast wind direction and speed* at your altitudes and finally the *Notices to Airmen (NOTAMS)* along your route.

The **Outlook** briefing contains a synopsis of what is expected to happen in general plus all the forecast data for your time of flight. Outlooks are for flights that will take place at least 6 hours after your briefing. Aviation forecast materials only go up to 48 hours in advance, and many of them only go 12 to 24 hours.

An **Abbreviated** briefing simply means that you have a specific question on one or two items. Say you want to know if the surface winds at your departure airport are going to be gusty, or if there are any Temporary Flight Restrictions from Indianapolis to Chicago. The briefer is still required to give you any Adverse Conditions over the area, but otherwise the only thing you will be given is what you ask for.

Chapter 11

Weather Brief Training for Student Pilots

"I am a new sport pilot instructor in Las Cruces. I would like to have my students call for a weather briefing before there lesson. So they can be comfortable with talking with flight service. Do you think this is ok with the work load that is on the briefer?" --LRU

I love having student pilots call me when they are first in training, and most of the people I work with are very patient with them when they identify themselves as a student up front. The instructor pilot is key to bringing students and ATC together, and there are ways that will help both start out on the right foot.

First of all, before the student ever is actually ready to get into an airplane and fly, most flight instructors do have them call the AFSS for a standard weather briefing in order to gain the experience. We can usually tell a student from the first words uttered. Not to mention the echo you hear since they usually call on a speakerphone.

Please make it a true "training" session. Get a printout of what current weather you can beforehand and separate it into the various groupings - Advisories, synopsis, current weather, forecast weather, winds and NOTAMs in that order.

If you pick the weather up at 5 minutes past the hour, then unless there is a "special" at your destination airport, it should be good until the top of the next hour, so you have 45 minutes to go over it with him or her yourself.

You ask "why should we go to all that trouble if you are going to brief him"? The reason is that you want the student to try and follow what we are saying visually. Also, if something prints out that looks funny, you can circle it and ask for clarification at the end of the brief.

As your student calls the AFSS, instruct him or her to tell us that they are a student, this keys the AFSS person to slow down a bit and be ready for questions.

Remember to have the student be ready with the data we need to input into the computer about the flight prior to the briefing. It impresses us when we do not have to guide the student through converting local time to Greenwich Mean Time (GMT) or Zulu. Many times the student is on the phone and as we ask for each item we hear the student call back over his shoulder "What's the type aircraft?....What altitude?" That really reflects poorly on the instructor.

Common student errors include such things as saying "Hi, I am 123-R-K" instead of November 1-2-3-Romeo-Kilo, or calling a Skyhawk a C-1-7-2 instead of a Cessna 172. I usually explain that aircraft types that begin with C are military cargo craft. Ensure that the student knows the identifiers for the airports and fixes enroute, and how to spell them phonetically if needed.

There are many things that you do automatically as a seasoned pilot that the student flounders through.

As the Briefer begins going through a standard briefing format, have the student follow where he is in the printed material. This allows the student to hear how the various weather contractions are stated aloud. When I know I am addressing a student, I tend to emphasize which items are written in MSL versus AGL, but if your briefer does not, then once the brief is over, be sure to query the student to make sure she understands the difference and why it is important.

Allow the Briefer to complete the briefing, then the student can ask them to back up and explain things. When Briefers are interrupted a lot during the brief, they could lose track of where what's been given and miss something. But do not hesitate to ask the Briefer to slow down if they are going too fast!

In general, if a student wants to have any lengthy explanations of weather systems and how they will affect a flight, unless it is for a flight that is imminent, we encourage the student to call after 7 pm, when our phone traffic slows down for the day. This courtesy ensures that pilots needing to get to their plane and go are not delayed. This is also a good time to ask about any other ATC related information the student may be confused about.

The website www.afss.com has some information about what exactly a flight service station does. Students frequently do not realize that the pilot briefer is the same guy who may be talking to him on the radio, or initiating search and rescue if he fails to show up.

Adverse Weather Conditions

Chapter 12

Preflight Weather Briefings

Part 1

The Standard Briefing - Adverse Conditions

Preflight briefings of any nature will always include adverse weather conditions. Right up front, the Briefer is telling you what are the worst atmospheric conditions that the National Weather Service (NWS) expects you to face enroute, and any other information pertinent to the flight. This also includes Temporary Flight Restrictions (TFR's) and any NOTAMs, or Notices to Airmen that have been issued for the destination airport which could keep an aircraft from landing.

In general, Airmen's Meteorological Statements or AIRMETS are weather advisories pertaining to cloud cover, visibility, turbulence and icing that could cause small to medium sized aircraft to alter or cancel their intended flights. Significant Meteorological Statements or SIGMETS are issued when conditions will strongly affect larger and stronger craft as well. Convective Sigmets (WSTs) relate to thunderstorms, and Area Weather Watches (AWW) are forecasted areas of Severe thunderstorms and tornados.

These advisories are issued by various offices of the National Weather Service routinely at specific times of the day. Should weather develop that was not forecast and it is noticed by a NWS official who is stationed at one of the Air Route Traffic Control Centers (ARTCC's), he may choose to issue a Center Weather Advisory or CWA. A CWA can cover any type of weather phenomena.

Temporary Flight Restrictions and NOTAMs will be covered in depth in a later chapter, the only ones given to the pilot up front are ones that would be critical for a pilot to know should the call be cut off before the end of the briefing. This includes destination airport closures or runway closures or special airspace restrictions.

This also includes any Presidential Temporary Flight Restrictions (TFR's). All other types of TFR's are included in the Notices to Airman (NOTAM) section of the brief. And the last of the adverse conditions relates to the NOTAMs at your destination airport. Because there is the possibility that the call could be cut off or end prior to getting to the NOTAM section, briefers are required to do a quick check up front to see if there is a NOTAM indicating a condition that would keep a pilot from landing at his destination.

Why are these up front? Because if you know that there is icing along the route you gave us, you may choose to stop right there and either ask us to look at alternate routes, or alternate times to fly. And, let's face it, if the airport is closed or if there is a Presidential TFR locking down the airport you want to fly into, that pretty well requires a change of plans.

Types of AIRMETS

(Airmen's Meteorological Information)

AIRMET SIERRA

IFR, Mountain Obscuration or Other Limitations to Visibility

IFR (Instrument Flight Rules) This AIRMET indicates that the area which has been defined by National Weather Service using a designated series of NAVAIDis likely to contain broken to overcast cloud conditions wherein the ceilings are lower than 1,000 feet AGL, and/or the Visibility is less than 3 miles. VFR (Visual Flight Rule) aircraft are not supposed to fly in these conditions, so the Briefer may follow this advisory with the statement "VFR not recommended".

Mountain Obscuration is only issued in areas of higher terrain, Mountain Obscuration indicates that the ceilings in the affected area are lower than 3,000 AGL, and/or visibilities are less than 5 miles – basically what is known as Marginal VFR or MVFR.

In a place where the ground is flat, MVFR is possible, but in the mountains there is granite hiding in the cumulus. This advisory also earns the statement "VFR not recommended" from a Briefer.

AIRMET TANGO

Turbulence, Sustained Surface Winds, and Low Level Wind Shear

AIRMET's for **turbulence** are issued when the NWS determines that there is potential for light to moderate turbulence throughout an area. The AIRMET will indicate the altitudes where the aircraft can expect to be shaken. Frequently there will be an AIRMET for turbulence that is surface based, and another one that is based aloft – usually in the jet stream levels.

Turbulence is classified as light, moderate, severe or extreme. A forecast for severe to extreme turbulence will be issued as a SIGMET.

Mountain Wave turbulence is caused by a strong wind flow perpendicular to a mountain range. The lifting air on the windward side of the mountain can flow upwards to altitudes above 35,000 feet, as they crest, the wave of air reverses and pushes downwards. These conditions can cause a pilot to gain and/or lose altitude rapidly.

AIRMET's for turbulence can also include cautionary statements concerning Low Level Wind Shear or LLWAS. Wind Shear occurs when there is a strong wind that rapidly changes direction near the surface, pushing and pulling the aircraft in unexpected directions. (See chapter entitled Wicked, Wicked Wind Shear) Wind shear may also occur within a few thousand feet of the surface – so that surface winds are only a few knots from one direction, but a thousand feet off the ground the direction changes and the speed increases by thirty knots.

Sustained Surface Winds -This AIRMET is issued when winds at the surface are expected to be 30 knots or greater for an extended period of time. This can also be a contributing factor to low ceilings and visibilities in blowing dust or sand.

AIRMET ZULU
ICING

When icing is expected to be trace or light, an AIRMET is issued. The AIRMET will state what altitudes you can expect to pick up some form of icing in a given area. The AIRMET will also indicate the base of the freezing levels and the forecast time period.

All AIRMET information is considered to be widespread because they must be forecast to affect an area of at least 3000 square miles at any one time. However, if the total area to be affected during the forecast period is very large, it could be that only a small portion of this total area would be affected at any one time.

AIRMETs are routinely issued for six hour periods beginning at 0245 UTC, and are amended as necessary due to changing weather conditions.

Types of SIGMETS

(Significant Meteorological Information)

Like AIRMETs, SIGMETs are considered to be widespread because they must be affecting or be forecast to affect an area of at least 3000 square miles at any one time. They.are issued for 4 hour periods. If conditions persist beyond the forecast period, the SIGMET is updated and reissued.

Turbulence

A SIGMET for turbulence indicates that severe to extreme turbulence could be a factor for your flight. This is usually caused by a particularly strong front at the surface or a very strong jet stream aloft. The SIGMET will specify what altitudes the turbulence is expected. Frequently the SIGMET will overlay portions of an AIRMET.

Icing

A SIGMET for icing is usually pretty bad news. This indicates severe icing is expected in an area – the kind that doubles the weight of your aircraft in short order and freezes your flaps. The SIGMET will advise you as to the altitudes the icing is expected to take place.

Sandstorm or Duststorm

When the surface winds are so high that visibilities are expected to be lower than three miles, a SIGMET is issued. Always surface based, the advisory will usually tell you how high the sand or dust is expected to affect your flight. This is not only important for visibility's sake, but for the amount of debris you could suck into the carburetor.

Volcanic Ash

Not usually a factor in the continental US – unless another Mt. St. Helens is expected to blow, volcanic ash also causes limited visibilities and offers a potential for engine damage. The advisory can include altitudes from the surface well into the flight levels.

The NWS will occasionally issue warnings about ash drift that is cause by the active volcanoes in the Aleutian chain and in Mexico.

SIGMETs associated with a hurricane are issued for a 6 hour period. All other SIGMETS are issued initially for 4 hours. If conditions persist beyond the forecast period, the SIGMET is updated and reissued.

CONVECTIVE SIGMETs
(WST)

WST advisories are issued hourly for thunderstorms greater than or equal to VIP level 4 affecting 40% or more of an area at least 3000 square miles.

They will also delineate areas where high VIP level thunderstorms are embedded in lower intensity rainshowers and where you can expect lines of thunderstorms. The WST will also note when the surface winds are expected to be greater than or equal to 50 knots, when the storms will generate hail at the surface greater than or equal to 3/4 inches in diameter, and tornadoes.

Any Convective SIGMET (WST) implies severe or greater turbulence, severe icing, low visibilities and low level wind shear. A WST may be issued for any convective situation which the forecaster feels is hazardous to all categories of aircraft. Convective Sigmets are issued five minutes before the hour. The text of the bulletin consists of either an observation and a forecast or just a forecast. The forecast is valid for 2 hours, but if a new WST is issued in an area, it supercedes the previous one. The WST will normally indicate if the conditions are building or dissipating.

The WST's are designated as **W** (western), **C** (central), or **E** (eastern) and are issued numerically beginning at 00:00 UTC daily. (i.e. WST 1C is the first one issued by the central region after 0000 Universal Coordinated Time)

Video Integrator Processor or VIP refers to a scale of precipitation intensity being measured by radar. There are 6 levels. Level 1 is very light precipitation and level 6 is very heavy with large hail possible. High levels of precipitation also indicate storm cloud tops. Level 1 precipitation can have tops as low as 15,000 feet MSL, where Level 6 can be above 55,000 feet

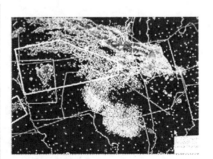

A Convective SIGMET is drawn in white over the RADAR display of a thunderstorm.

The area covered by a Convective SIGMET is described by NWS designated aviation fixes – usually VORTACs or airport designators. The storms may be in lines, usually connected with frontal movement. There can also be a large area containing an unorganized scattering of storms of varying intensity covering several states. This happens frequently in the summertime when the afternoon heating combines with ambient moisture flowing aloft at midlevels – which are altitudes between the surface and the altitude containing only frozen ice particles.

Area Weather Watches (AWW)
Severe Storm Warning

Although the NWS issues Severe Storm and Tornado Warnings, your Briefer will only give you information on official Severe Thunderstorm Watches or Tornado Watches.

A Warning indicates that severe weather is possible given the meteorological conditions in the area. A Watch indicates that the severe weather indicated is imminent or already occurring.

The AWW's are numbered by year and include the words "Severe Storm" or "Tornado" in the first line. The trapezoidal or rectangular area is described by using a distance either side of a line that is described with both civilian locations (40 west of Abiline) and by aviation identifiers (40 w ABI). For Example:

WW 204 SEVERE TSTM OK TX 172000Z - 180300Z
                    AXIS..50 STATUTE MILES EAST AND WEST OF LINE..
                    35NNE CQB/CHANDLER OK/ - 30SW FTW/FORT WORTH TX/
                    ..AVIATION COORDS.. 45NM E/W /38W TUL - 42WSW DFW/
                    HAIL SURFACE AND ALOFT 2 INCHES.WIND GUSTS 60
                    KNOTS. MAX TOPS TO 500. MEAN STORM MOTION VECTOR 24035.

The Flight Service computer overlays a diagram of the AWW on a map, which allows the Briefers to determine if a pilot's proposed route of flight will intersect the area.

Center Weather Advisories (CWA)

When the other NWS units fail to recognize a condition as being widespread enough to warrant issuing one of the previously given advisories, the meteorologist on duty at the ARTCC will put out a CWA. This advisory is within the boundaries of the Center's airspace and can describe any weather condition affecting flight.

Portions of a CWA can include a Meteorological Impact Statement (MIS). This part is for ATC planning purposes only and is not given to pilots during a briefing. It gives a synopsis of weather patterns pertaining just to that Center's airspace and how that weather could become a factor in the future.

Other Weather Advisories

Sometimes weather advisories related to micro-climates will be issued by a local NWS office. For instance, a cold front just east of the Sandia mountain pass may funnel high winds directly to Albuquerque International Airport (ABQ) , so the NWS will issue a High Wind advisory only for that airport. Even though Double Eagle Airport (AEG) lies just 20 miles west of ABQ, they will not be affected by the wind flow. Nor will Sandia Airpark (1N1) nor Moriarty Airport (0E0) which lie on the east (windward) side of the mountain.

This type of advisory may be sent to Flight Service and the Tower, but is not generally available to Online aviation websites. The information is also sent to local media for broadcast. You will find indications of the expected wind velocities in the Terminal Forecast or TAF.

Winter Ice – Beautiful and Deadly

I woke up one Thanksgiving morning and looked outside – there was snow on the ground! My first thought was, wow, it's early this year! My second thought was, am I ready for this?

Are you ready for this? As pilots you know what needs to be done for your aircraft in the winter. How do you plan for bad weather? What products does the National Weather Service have that can give you a clue as to what to expect?

As temperature begin to slide lower, the probability of airframe icing increases. Suddenly the light fluffy clouds of summertime take on a more sinister aspect. AIRMETs for icing are being issued and the base of the freezing level lowers daily.

Throughout ATC, specialists are required to review training materials on how icing affects aircraft and what procedures should be used to help the pilot avoid it. When you obtain your briefing from flight services, the briefer will make sure you are aware of any weather advisories for icing.

INTENSITY   **ICE ACCUMULATION**

Trace   Ice becomes perceptible. Rate of accumulation slightly greater than rate of sublimation. It is not hazardous even though deicing/anti-icing equipment is not utilized, unless encountered for an extended period of time (over 1 hour).

Light   The rate of accumulation may create a problem if flight is prolonged in this environment (over 1 hour). Occasional use of deicing/anti-icing equipment removes/prevents accumulation. It does not present a problem if the deicing/anti-icing equipment is used.

Moderate The rate of accumulation is such that even sort encounters become potentially hazardous and use of deicing/anti-icing or diversion is necessary.

Severe   The rate of accumulation is such that deicing/anti-icing equipment fails to reduce or control the hazard. Immediate diversion is necessary.

An AIRMET is a weather advisory issued by the National Weather Service (NWS) for hazardous conditions which are expected to affect small to medium sized aircraft – ones with little or no anti-icing capability. SIGMETs warn of reported conditions dangerous to all aircraft.

The other things that will affect your flight are the freezing level and the presence of visible moisture (clouds or rain). Surface observations, satellite photos and radar combine to give you a good mental picture of altitudes and locations to avoid. Pilot reports are a significant aid that can only be offered from one pilot to the others. Weather advisories predict icing, but pilot reports confirm it.

Most icing occurs between the freezing level to 10 degrees below freezing. Colder than that and you are flying through snow – the precipitation has already taken a form that will slide past the aircraft rather than stick to it.

Since the standard atmospheric lapse rate is 2 degrees per thousand feet, it is normally suggested to descend to escape freezing altitudes. One situation that defies this parameter occurs when an aircraft is flying through an inversion layer near a warm front overriding colder air. Rain falling from the warm layer above falls through the colder air below becoming supercooled.

An aircraft penetrating the rain is quickly coated in hard clear ice and should either ascend to the warmer air above or turn out of the precipitation quickly. This scenario is seen frequently in the first half of winter around the Great Lakes. Air slides south from Canada warming and becoming moisture filled from the lakes. As it slides over the frozen surface to the south/southeast the air condenses and releases rain into the colder airmass over the land. Known as Lake Effect icing, it can be a real killer.

Make it a habit from November through March to always be aware of freezing levels – if you need help, call flight service for a pilot brief before the flight.

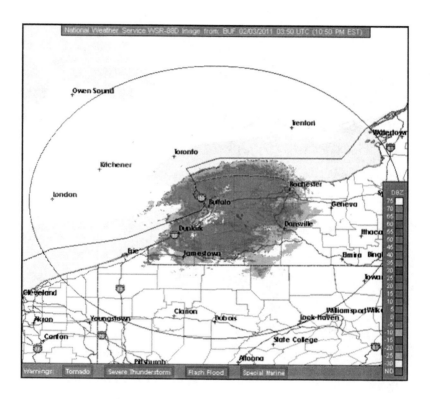

Image taken 2/2/2011 from www.aviationweather.com website, Radar Mosaic.
Notice that shading indicates a relatively low DBZ, which in summer would
indicate thick clouds but not much moisture. In winter the widespread area of
greys indicated moderate to severe icing possible.

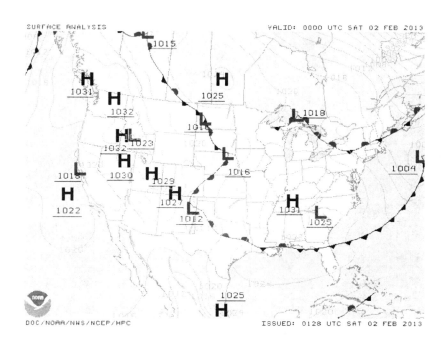

Standard Weather Briefing Part 2

- The Synopsis

The synopsis is really an overview of the fronts, highs, lows and other meteorological events that are the basis for the kind of weather a pilot will be flying through. Many pilots consider this to be an unnecessary part of the brief – they just want to know what the weather is – not the underlying factors that are creating it. And to be honest, some of the Briefers are really into the meteorological part of it to the point that they can drone on past what a pilot actually needs.

This is not to say that the synopsis is unimportant – hardly! Knowing what is causing turbulence, IFR, or thunderstorms gives you a big clue how to avoid it, go around it or when it will be over.

A good example is turbulence. An atmospheric disturbance aloft will cause turbulence to stick around all day and night, but if the turbulence is due to daily heating of the earth's surface, it's a good bet that it will disappear as the evening's coolness sets in.

Later in the Flight Service portion of the book we will discuss Climates and Microclimates in more detail – these will give you a broader idea as to how geography and meteorology contribute to the flight conditions in a given area.

Here are a few common synopsis:

"A Dry Stable Airmass" – this is music to the pilot's ears. No rain, no clouds, no really turbulent conditions, just clear skies.

Words like Cold Front or Warm Front should invoke instant alarms in a VFR pilot's mind. They usually engender low cloud conditions in general, and frontal thunderstorms frequently create cloud bases at only 2 thousand feet or lower. Frontal activity is highest over the far Northwest or in the Midwest and Eastern U.S.

A "Marine Layer" can sit over the coast for weeks keeping the coastline covered in low clouds (IFR) daily until noon or later.

"Mid-Level Moisture and Diurnal Heating" This is the standard recipe for the southwestern part of the U.S. during the months of July and August. It means that every morning the skies are clear and every afternoon there are thunderstorms somewhere. The thunderstorms are usually in a different place every day, and they dry up and blow away a few hours after sunset.

Standard Weather Briefing - Part 3
VNR Statement

"VFR Not Recommended" is a phrase that the Flight Service people are famous for. Most pilots figure that Briefers eagerly practice saying it in front of a mirror wearing a Freddie Kruger mask.

Pilot Briefers are supposed to state "VFR Not Recommended" (VNR) whenever there are AIRMETS in place for IFR over the plains, and Mountain Obscuration wherever there may be cumulus granite raking the sky. It is also given to VFR pilots who designate a route of flight that takes them through thunderstorms. Briefers can also give the VNR statement when there are no advisories, but he has observed that low cloud ceilings and visibilities are present through surface and pilot reports.

Since Briefer's are taught to be cautious, some pilots become frustrated when the VNR statement is used. They call us "Fright Service" and boast how they have had great flights after their briefings. These are the pilots who begin to ignore warnings and one day find themselves in conditions they cannot handle while flying VFR. Briefer's are not omniscient, but they are doing their best to give pilots all the data they need for a safe flight.

Using the VNR statement is supposed to be at the discretion of the Briefer, so if there is an advisory – but it is hours old and the Briefer has seen on his satellites and current conditions that the condition no longer exists, he may omit it during the Brief.

FRIGHT SERVICE!!!

Sometimes Flight Service gives a briefing and it seems that the pilot just plain isn't listening. In the past (in a less politically correct era) those of us who really care about the pilots sometimes might make the following "wake-up" remarks. These are usually given to small aircraft who are adamantly going to fly into REALLY bad weather and/or terrain.

· Can I have the name of your next of kin?

· Before you take off, can I be added as a beneficiary to your life insurance?

· Sir, do you understand the term "Cumulus Granite" ?

· La Junta FSS – "Sir, on departure please contact Trinidad radio with a pilot report – I don't want to be the last person to talk to you."

My personal favorite was given by a Briefer known as Pappy at Monroe Flight Service to a student pilot who later went on to become a Flight Service Specialist.

…"You keep your G—D— Ass on the ground! You don't need to be flying in this mess!"

Standard Weather Briefing ‑ Part 4
Current Conditions

The Current Conditions portion of your Standard Briefing will contain information derived from several sources. It contains primarily the surface conditions at your departure and destination, altitude appropriate sky conditions enroute plus radar and satellite data.

If there are rain and thunderstorms involved, the Briefer will describe the current position of the storms, their intensity and direction of movement. In the Adverse Conditions portion of the Brief, the pilot has received the Convective SIGMETS and Area Weather Watches, now the Briefer will relate the actual positions of the radar returns to the forecast data.

Satellite data can show overshooting tops for imminent thunderstorms, or the retreating edge of a low cloud or fog layer.

The Briefer's "Bible" — FAA publication JO 7110.10, tells him to "summarize" all the available data, though most Briefers will give the current METAR from your departure and destination stations, and simply summarize all the stations in between. The METAR is a coded report of surface conditions. It includes surface winds in degrees and knots, the cloud heights in Above Ground Level measurements (AGL), the visibilities in statute miles, and the temperature and dewpoint in degrees Celcius. The altimeter is in inches of mercury, but 29.92 inches will be read as two-niner-niner-two in separate digits.

When the Briefer states the cloud heights, he will use the same phraseology that you will use to tell ATC your altitude. The altitudes are stated in thousands with altitudes over 10,000 feet stated in separate digits – 10,000 is stated one-zero thousand, or 25,000 is written 250, but stated as two-five thousand.

The cloud decks are stated as few (FEW), scattered (SCT), broken (BKN) or overcast (OVC). Broken and overcast are considered ceilings. MVFR or marginal VFR conditions exist when ceilings are at or below 3,000 feet AGL. IFR ceilings are at or below 1,000 feet AGL Visibilities also play a factor. If the visibility is at or below 3 miles, the reporting point is considered to be IFR. It is LIFR (Low IFR) when visibilities are 1 mile or less.

When reporting a METAR to a pilot, the Briefer will usually give the surface temperature so that the pilot can determine Density Altitude. The Briefer is only required to include the dewpoint if there is a difference of 5 degrees or less than the temperature. This is because the close temperature/dewpoint spread could indicate that fog or rain is present or likely to occur.

The METAR will contain information on current weather at the station as well, such as rain, snow, blowing dust and mist. The remarks section should also contain information as to when precipitation began or ended during the previous hour, and the direction in which the storms have moved. This is also where you will see reports stating such things as "mountain tops obscured all quadrants".

Enroute the METARs will be summarized. If the cloud ceilings are consistent over a large area then change later it may sound like this:

"Ceilings broken to overcast four to five thousand from Indianapolis to

Louisville, from Louisville to Nashville ceilings overcast between three thousand and three thousand five hundred.   Light rain being reported throughout southern Indiana through Tennessee."

The Briefer also scans the Pilot Reports (UA's) to see if any of them were given affecting the altitudes in and around which you will be flying. Pilot reports are observations of flying conditions given to radio by pilots already airborne.   The importance of Pilot Reports cannot be overstated.

METARs WITHIN A 50NMR TAKEN WITHIN 10 MINUTES

KGLD 310302Z AUTO 30014G31KT 3SM +TSRA BR BKN020 BKN070 OVC095 18/16 A3022 RMK AO2 PK WND 28031/0254 LTG DSNT ALQDS

KSYF 310255Z AUTO 00000KE 10 RA SCT007 SCT019 BKN080 19/17 A3018

KCBK 310255Z 12003KT 10 CLR 27/17 A3009

KITR 210304Z AUTO 07015KT 10 –RA BKN110 19/16/A3014 RMK LTG DSNT ALQDS TSE0258 PRESFR

- *"San Angelo Radio, N3RK just east of Marfa, with a*
- *pilot report, over"*
-
- *"N3RK, San Angelo Radio, go ahead pilot report"*

- *"N3RK is a Cherokee at one one thousand five*
  hundred, we have had moderate turbulence from
  El Paso to Marfa, and just started getting some
  severe jolts as we got closer to Marfa, we
  descended to seven thousand five hundred and are
  just getting some light turbulence at this altitude"

Pilot Reports

Ahh, the lowly pilot report. With every briefing you receive from flight service, we always ask for pilot reports. Pilot reports are the missing pieces of a puzzle in the realm of Weather Service measurements and instrumentation.

The weatherman is chained to the ground with his computers and calculations. He has satellites far above the atmosphere to give him a look at airflow there, and he has surface observation stations feeding data into the computers below the atmosphere, but except for weather balloons sent aloft a couple times a day, he has no way of knowing what is happening IN the atmosphere. It is still one of the greatest guessing games known to man – what is going to happen next?

Enter the pilot report. Pilots cleave the air at altitudes from just above the surface nearly to the ozone layer every day. They do not just see weather, they become a part of it. The data that they accumulate and give to air traffic gets fed immediately into National Weather Service databases. This data confirms or disputes the forecasts made to that point and it serves as the basis for the next educated guess as to how the weather will affect the people, animals, crops, roadbuilders, campers, golfers and pilots.

Pilot reports are a pilot's best source of weather on his route. AIRMETs and SIGMETs are issued, but are conditions they forecast really there? Is there really icing in those clouds over Indianapolis? A Cessna Skyhawk pilot is anxious to get home to Cincinnati. The AIRMET exists, but what is really happening? During his briefing he finds that the pilot of a Beechcraft Baron flying from Terre Haute to Dayton reported a trace of rime icing at FL115, but after dropping to FL075 and the Baron reported clear with an outside temperature of plus 4 degrees C.

The Skyhawk pilot leaves immediately and comfortably makes it home.

On the other hand, if the Baron had reported that he had encountered light icing from FL045 on up to FL115, the Skyhawk pilot, who had no de-icing equipment on board, would probably take a hotel room for the night and try again tomorrow.

AIRMETs are indications that certain types of flying hazards are probable in an area, but a Pilot Report is real-time information that is of incredible value to other pilots. When a pilot report is received, it is considered pertinent for briefing purposes for only one hour. After that time it is removed from the weather service products, insuring that the only data the pilots and briefers receive is current.

It is not thrown out completely though. This data is accumulated with other pilot reports and used to reconsider advisory products. The pilots themselves therefore frequently initiate action on the part of the Weather Service to stimulate the issuance of AIRMETs or SIGMETs.

All pilot reports, even the negative ones have value. If it is forecast to be turbulent, but all the pilots are reporting smooth flying conditions – this is Good! If it is forecast to be smooth and clear and the pilot reports it is smooth and clear – this is Good! All pilot reports are valuable.

Every time you give a pilot report Flight Service needs your location, type aircraft and altitude to start with. After that you should give whatever clues to the big puzzle that you can. Are you in the clouds at your altitude? What altitude did you enter them at? How thick is the layer? How many miles can you see in front of you?

At your altitude are you getting turbulence or icing? What intensity? Do you see any rain in the area? The weather service likes having pilots give wind speed/direction and temperature aloft data in pilot reports.

The two categories that tend to confuse a lot of pilots are the intensities and types of turbulence and icing. Icing is a little more obvious. If it is barely visible it is trace. If it is lightly coating all surfaces it is "light". If it looks like thick icing on a birthday cake and is starting to make flying difficult, it is moderate. If it is severe, you are probably already losing altitude so fast that you don't have time for a pilot report.

Air carriers define turbulence according to passenger discomfort. Light turbulence causes coffee in those little Styrofoam cups to slosh around a bit. Moderate turbulence means the coffee slops out of the cup and may tip the cup over. Severe turbulence lands the coffee in the lap of the guy in the next seat back, and extreme turbulence tosses the stewardess into the lap of the guy in the next seat back.

Sometimes the turbulence is classified as "chop". Ever drive down a dirt road that has a lot of parallel ridges like an old time washboard? That is chop.

There are a lot of interesting comments that are added to pilot reports which will bring home a condition in a more personal way. One pilot was reporting nasty headwinds and turbulence. The report read:
TCS UA/OV ONM-TCS/TM 2219/FL085/TP C152/WV 180045/ TB MOD/ RM "Only thing moving in this aircraft is my stomach".

Or this one in southeastern New Mexico:

CNMUA/OVCNM/TM0245/FL065/TPC210/TBMOD-SEV/RMITS
ROUGHERTHANACORNCOBUPHERE

My favorite was made by an unheated Experimental flying from El Paso to Albuquerque up the Rio Grande in February. He reported the temperature, then said, "I should have worn my fur-lined jock strap." Unfortunately, the supervisor would not let me code that one into the database unedited.

Flight Service is the primary way ATC wants to take and disseminate pilot reports. If you give one to the Towers, they will pass it on to Flight Service because the Tower computers are not linked directly to the Weather service.

Center controllers have no requirement to take pilot reports, and if you try to give them one they may simply have you contact Radio.

Other, more unusual, pilot reports can include such things as seeing the ground obscured by blowing sand or dust, and then giving the dust tops, or observing a forest fire where there are no TFR's already in the area. This is one of the ways that the Forest Service gets on top of fires quickly in the more remote regions.

How to Give a Pilot Report That is Truly Appreciated

At one point in time I listened over the console as a pilot gave a co-worker what can only be labeled as the "pilot report from hell".

Mind you, we want pilot reports (PIREP). They are frequently the only way we can verify forecasts and give pilots the information they really need about conditions aloft. But when a pilot starts rambling on and on with cute, folksy conversation and often extensive descriptions and phrasing about what he sees— we have a real problem coding the information into the computer.

Here's an example:

Radio, this is N123 with a pilot report....I'm a turbo two ten RG161 over Whoachi Lake, VFR and we're gettin' bumped around quite a bit. We can see a cloud deck way up north and looks like there might be some rain up that way with some flashes..and back when we took off out of Podunk it was hazy and clouds were about nine thousand, right now we've got some clouds above us, but it's clear at our altitude but real cold!

If someone gives you a pilot report like that – how in the heck do you put it into the computer in a format that others can understand?

A PIREP like that takes between 10 and 15 minutes of radio time. We would have to ask the pilot such things as What altitude?, Where is he in reference to airports or official navigational aids? Are the clouds scattered, broken or overcast? Then we have to figure out how many pilot reports to encode since he talks about both current and past portions of the flight.

In the meantime, the guy working Radio may have a couple pilots on other frequencies trying to activate or cancel flight plans and a Lifeguard needing an IFR clearance from a small remote airport. Remember, each radio specialist is listening to 50 or more frequencies.

In this case we would recommend that the pilot should have given a pilot report for haze tops and cloud bases shortly after take-off. Then as he began encountering the turbulence and other good information – give radio another, more pertinent call.

95

Here is an example of a useful Pilot Report:

Albuquerque Radio, N123 with a Pilot Report.

- (Pause while the guy on radio has a chance to open the PIREP form)

- *N123, Albuquerque Radio, Go ahead.*

- *N123 is a C172 on the Roswell 290 degree radial at 40 miles at niner thousand five hundred. We have light chop, temperature is minus 2, scattered clouds above around 25,000. We can see lower clouds and lightening north.*

This is easy to input and another pilot getting briefed can look at the report as it is encoded below and know exactly what this pilot wanted others to know.

ROW UA TM/2134 OV/ROW290040 TP/C172 FL/095 SK/SCT250 TB/LGT CHOP TA/M02 RM/LOWER CLOUDS AND LTG N

Sometimes a pilot will call and say he wants to file a pilot report. He gives his location and type aircraft as requested and then says "It was a beautiful flight". This does not really tell us anything. If we assume that he means skies clear and negative turbulence, we are assuming this guy is not a thrill taker. Heck, for all we know he's an acrobatic pilot who thinks "Beautiful flight" means he got the guy in the right seat to puke

Some pilots feel compelled to lump a whole flight's worth of complicated data into one pilot report at the end of the flight. If a Bonanza landing Tucson took off from Texas 2 hours ago – his climbout experience is no longer pertinent. Pilot reports are kept for only one hour in order to have the most useful and accurate information. We would have loved to have that data – two hours ago!

If the weather is bad, then giving multiple pilot reports along the route is really helpful. When possible, give one within half an hour of take-off, and perhaps another enroute. Then give us one when you land and close your flight plan about the conditions during descent.

Please use the standard phraseology – this way everyone knows how to interpret the information. The basic information needed for a pilot report begins with the aircraft type, location, and altitude. Only one of the optional fields needs to be added, and standard phraseology is best.

The optional PIREP fields are:

Sky Conditions – Cloud bases and tops or sky clear. Clouds are few, scattered, broken or overcast.

Turbulence – Negative, Light, Moderate, Severe or Extreme (NOT Smooth, "a little bit" or "I was picking my teeth off the ceiling") This can include the words Chop, Intermittent, Continuous, or Occasional.

Air Temperature – in Celsius please. This field is mandatory when giving an icing report.

Wind Vector – Direction and Speed. You can say "southwest at 10 knots" and we will encode it as 24010kt. Please do not say "On the nose at 10 knots", because we can't see what direction your nose is pointed.

Icing – Trace, Light, Moderate or Severe – along with Rime, Clear, or Mixed. You can give a range of altitudes if you climbed through the icing. Frequently a pilot will say they incurred "some" icing, or "a bunch". Always remember that an icing report must include temperature.

Weather – This broad category includes inflight visibility, and limitations to visibility such as dust storms or haze, and includes all forms of precipitation. Always give visibilities in whole numbers.

Remarks – Whatever doesn't fit anywhere else. Includes reports of Thunderstorms at a distance, comments such as During Descent or

"Tossed Dog into back seat". There are only 77 characters allowed in this field – so please keep it to the point.

In general, a flight service specialist will listen to what is said, then try to encode it properly. She or he may read back what they've encoded to verify your meaning. When you give a range of information, they are required to submit whatever is the worst value.

If a pilot says that the bases of the overcast are four to five thousand, Radio will encode four thousand. If you say the temperature is between minus two and minus three, they will encode minus three.

If you want to give extensive data, the specialist may be forced to split it into two pilot reports. Please be patient as he or she will need to take the time to get it all into the pilot report mask, then read it back to you for verification. If you want some more information on PIREP encoding, check out section 7-1-20 of the Airmen's Information Manual.

Pilot Reports are our best way of communicating timely and useful weather data to other pilots, and you can help by giving us the data in a way that is easy to understand.

Reading the Radar

The capabilities of weather radar these days is amazing. Even more amazing are the programs used to interpret the data brought in by the raw radar. With today's programs you can see not just storm intensities and movement, you can see windflow even when there is no precipitation in an area.

Weather radar, unlike Air Traffic Radar, was originally designed to see moisture. An individual site measures the amount of moisture and how far up in the atmosphere the moisture extends within its small area. Because upward development is what occurs when thunderstorms are created, the higher up the moisture extends usually equates to the severity of the other weather elements, such as wind and hail, associated with that moisture. The radar site also shows how quickly the parcel of moisture is moving across the observed area.

One radar site alone will only see about a hundred miles out at best, and the outer fringe moisture levels will not be painted as accurately as those closer to the site. The National Weather Service has placed their radar sites across most of the nation close enough together that today's computers can weave the data from these sites together to form a "mosaic" of weather conditions. This is what you are looking at when you see the evening news and on most of the radars available to the public on the internet.

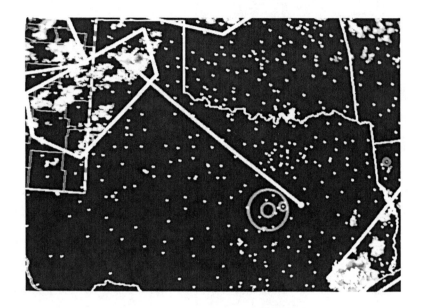

This RADAR picture shows that the pilot's flight starts out in clear skies east of the DFW area, but his destination in the Texas Panhandle is covered with Thunderstorms.   The colors of the radar returns indicate the severity of the storms, though the book only has a black and white rendition. The white outlines indicate a Convective SIGMET (WST) has been issued for the area.

Aviation Weather Advisory Circular AC 00-45

Vcp:32 DBZ	
75	H
70	V
65	Y
60	
55	
50	
45	M
40	O
35	D
30	
25	
20	
15	L
10	G
5	T
0	
-5	
-10	
-15	V
-20	L
-25	G
-30	T
ND	

Radar Depictions of Storm Levels

___ An acronym for Video Integrator and Processor. This processor was used on the WSR-57 and WSR-74C radars to indicate rainfall rates. It is still used occasionally on WSR-88D radar products. This processor contours radar reflectivity (in dBZ) into six VIP levels.

___ Categorized intervals of reflectivity which are computer processed by a Digital Video Integrator Processor (D/VIP). These intervals were very important before the installation of the 88-D Radar network. Some of the 88-D Radar products still have these intervals on them. The following table illustrates the various rainfall rates associated with VIPs:

VIP 1 (Level 1, 18-30 dBZ) Light precipitation
VIP 2 (Level 2, 30-38 dBZ) Light to Moderate Rain
VIP 3 (Level 3, 38-44 dBZ) Light to Moderate Rain
VIP 4 (Level 4, 44-50 dBZ) Moderate Rain
VIP 5 (Level 5, 50-57 dBZ) Moderate to Heavy Rain
VIP 6 (Level 6, >57 dBZ)   Heavy Rain

This book will not go into the technical aspects of radar sites or specific intensity levels produced by the radar sites, those interested can find specific information on NWS radars in their aviation weather guide – government publication AC-0045. You can find it online by typing this publication number in the search engine at www.nws.gov.

If you use the www.aviationweather.gov site you can pull up a national picture of radar that is very sensitive. It actually picks up cloud activity and around the center of the radar site it may on occasion pick up the tops of buildings and trees. Radar waves can bend with the right atmospheric conditions, so seeing what is called "anomalous propagation" (AP) is most prevalent after nightfall as the air cools. AP tends to hide any lower cloud or lighter precipitation if it is in the area, so you have to check the satellites to see if the radar returns are real or just the local skyline.

By opening up the national radar mosaic on that site it will expand the area so that even if there are no returns showing when it is small, anything that is there will pop up to be seen. Looping it gives you a better idea as to which direction the activity is moving and whether it is growing or dissipating.

The more dramatic colors – reds and oranges indicate some pretty severe thunderstorms. These are more often seen in summer and fall. Widespread areas of green and yellow are light to moderate precipitation. Blue is usually heavy cloud activity and pale gray means the computer is picking up something but isn't quite sure what.

Radar has a harder time picking up snow and ice than it does rain. During the winter time the blues and greys take on a more sinister reading. Even a pale cloud of grey could mean there is light precip in the area – and flying through it could cause ice accumulation. A smudge of light to deep blue can mean more significant icing is possible or that a small intense snowstorm is blowing through an area. Just because it is small does not mean it is harmless.

If you are using WSI or some other private vendor for your radar products the colors may be altered by their computers – in many cases they will show winter radars that have green for rain, pink for a rain/ice mix, and blue for snow. The worst thing you can fly through is a rain/ice mix – that is where you catch the heaviest icing on an aircraft. Be sure to become familiar with the variations of each different weather vendors radar interpretations.

Many of today's radar sites are also capable of producing a picture of the windflow over the site at altitudes from a hundred feet off the surface to well into the flight levels. The VAD is a National Weather Service (NWS) radar product little used in fixed wing aviation, but familiar to balloonists or anyone flying low. It is a tool that pilots and flight service specialists can use to provide critical information concerning low level wind shear and provides data about changes in wind flow patterns during a climb to higher altitudes.

Like normal weather radar, the VAD takes readings from precipitation, but the sensitivity of this instrument also reads tiny dust particles floating aloft. It can sense planes, birds, and butterflies as well, though its purpose is to reveal patterns over a given point. This means that any life form or aircraft picked up for just a moment in time does not normally affect the display. One exception to this is the seasonal or diurnal migration of large flocks of birds, which can alter the VAD readings at lower altitudes.

A VAD wind readout is measured in AGL altitudes at thousand foot increments. What an amateur will see the first time is what looks like an excel spreadsheet full of checkmarks with extra ticks. Those familiar with the NWS wind flow charts will see that each indicator, or flag, is actually pointing in the direction the wind is flowing towards. It is aligned with standard compass headings so that if it points up, wind flow is from south to north. It does not provide a specific direction in degrees.

The VAD display shows the winds at the MSL levels. For instance, ABQ VAD display does not even begin until 6,000 feet - because the surface there is 5,340. The Amarillo site starts with 1,000 - but the first 4,000 is always ND (no data) for the same reason.

The tick marks on the tail are speed measurements. A full tick is 10 knots, a half tick is five knots. A triangular sail at the end of the tick indicates fifty knots. At the bottom of the page are times listed in Greenwich Mean Time or GMT. Each reading is six minutes apart. The wind/speed indicators above indicate what was observed at that moment in time by the radar.

As long as there is something floating in the air, the VAD will read it. Sometimes the VAD has no readings. At the surface up to about 12,000 feet no readings indicate that winds are calm, but if there are winds — even strong winds above 15,000 feet, the VAD may have no return simply because of a lack of particulate matter floating about.

The VAD is used extensively for ballooning. During the Balloon Fiesta in Albuquerque each year, there is a competition wherein the participants must launch their balloons at least one mile away from the balloon field, then attempt to catch the correct winds to float over the field. On top of a 20 foot pole is the key to a brand new car. Whoever gets the key wins the car!

Fixed wing aircraft can benefit in areas where a high windshear potential exists. In southern California during a Santa Ana windflow, the surface winds can be almost dead calm, but within 500 feet the wind from the northeast can be ripping along at 30 to 40 knots. Checking the VAD wind readings in the area can provide the data needed to anticipate the sudden onset.

VAD winds can also point out potential problems in mountain passes. Pilots know to watch out for and avoid roll clouds and altocumulus standing lenticulars (ACSL) when they are trying to keep away from shearing, but when there is not enough moisture present, these visual indicators may not be available. This is a good time to call Flight Watch and request any VAD wind readouts in the area.

To access VAD wind readouts at home there are a couple options. One is www.weatherunderground.com. At the top, look for NEXRAD. Click on that, it will show a U.S. map with crosses wherever there is a radar site.

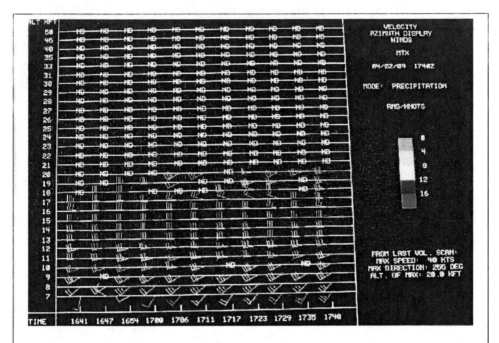

VAD Wind RADAR Readout

VAD winds update approximately every 6 minutes. The flags point in the direction the wind is blowing to. The tick marks are indications of speed, each tick is 10 knots, each half tick is 5 knots. The numbers to the left are MSL altitudes in thousands of feet. The flag at the lowest right corner is showing that at 1740 zulu at 7,000 MSL the wind was out of the southwest at 25 knots.

Click on the one where you want to see the radar. When the radar comes up, on the left edge of the picture a long thin bar reads "advanced radar types." Click there, then at the bottom of the list click on Velocity Azimuth Display to see a current readout.

A simpler method is available at www.pilotsandweather.com – on the top of the first page after logging in there is a box labeled 2D-WX. The symbol on the far right takes you straight to a VAD wind display. You do have to sign up for the service.

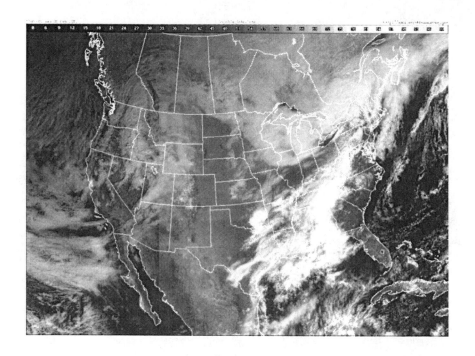

Visual Satellite Picture – dawn is just breaking on the west coast

Satellites - A Bird's Eye View

I lay back on my lawn chair one night marveling at the clarity of the milky way in the high desert night sky when I saw something moving strangely. Pointing it out to my friend, Karlis, I commented that is was going too fast to be an airplane, but way too slow for a comet!

Karlis looked at me and said, "I see it, it's a satellite."

Amazingly clear, the polar satellite moved out of the north and disappeared into the cluster of stars to the south. This type of satellite orbits in a path that closely follows the Earth's meridian lines, passing over the north and south poles once each revolution. Polar satellites circle at a fairly low altitude at about 850 km. This means that polar satellites can photograph clouds from closer than the high altitude geostationary satellites. Polar satellites, therefore, provide more detailed information about violent storms and cloud systems.

There are two types of satellite pictures that are returned to the National Oceanic and Atmospheric Administration (NOAA) offices for meteorological use, visible and infrared. For the rest of this article, I hope you can get to a computer and follow me in a tour of what those images can offer.

Start by going to website www.aviationweather.gov. On the left side bar you will see "Satellite", click on it and then on United States. Initially the dots above the U.S. map will say "visible" and "Latest Image". If you click on the word "Contiguous U.S.", you will get the most recent picture of the cloud conditions over the U.S. You can also click on one of the other boxes to get something closer to where you are now.

Go back to the main page and click on "visible" and "Loop-Big". Then click in the map somewhere again. After a few seconds to load, you will be able to see a continuous loop of what is happening. The beauty of the visible satellite is that you can see the wind flow patterns and how they affect the clouds beneath. Frequently you can follow multiple layers crisscrossing in perpendicular directions.

Jet stream activity produces long streaks across broad areas-generally west to east with some north-south variations. Low level moisture may move as a mass below that in a different direction, say from the gulf northwards. Fog shows up as a medium gray thick blob that does not move at all, but does thin out at the edges as the day progresses. Look for it in the San Joaquin valley of southern California or blanketing the northeast coast in the early evenings. Pilots who want to fly into a foggy area, and have been waiting for it to lift, can check the satellite data regularly to see if is beginning to thin.

Fluffy white puff balls geysering upwards, herald the formation of thunderstorms. This is mostly apparent in the mid to late summer afternoons. The speed at which they develop can be fascinating.

In summer, the National Weather Service (NWS) predicts thunderstorms virtually every day over the southwest. They know there is enough moisture and enough heat, and that the mountains will play a part in determining location, but the exact spot where today's storms will develop is the question. Watching the visible satellite gives us a clue.

Visible satellites also show the terminator as it travels across the land – this is the line between sunlight and darkness. You can usually see White Sands National Monument as a bright white dot in south central New Mexico, and if the skies are clear, morning and evening shadows delineate the Grand Canyon. When a large wildfire is reported raging across west Texas, you can see streaks of smoke.

The drawback to the visible satellite of course is darkness. At night the infrared satellites give us a look at cloud activity by sensing the temperature of moisture at various altitudes and displaying the data in shades of gray.

When you are planning a flight a week in advance, the satellites give you a pretty good indication of what is coming towards you. Keeping in mind that planetary rotation causes most systems to drift from west to east across the U.S. you can see what other pressures are coming to bear. If clouds off the west coast seem to be moving in a counterclockwise pattern, they will bring low and mid level moisture into California and the southwest in the next few days. Clouds moving in a line indicate the leading edge of a front, while random but relatively stationary clouds that build into thunderstorms then die in place show ambient moisture trapped in a high pressure system. That pattern will repeat daily until a strong front comes along to move the moisture out – usually in September.

Large areas of dry air are black or dark gray – this is really good flying weather. This area will also generally drift from west to east – giving you a heads up for the days to come. Strong bands of white clouds in Northern Canada moving south push rain into the great lakes and New England in the summer and blizzards in the winter.

Back at the main satellite page, notice a line on top that says *International imagery on ICAO projections*. Clicking on that will allow you to choose what part of the world you would like to see. The NWS keeps a close eye on the Atlantic ocean during hurricane season. Most of these are IR images only and do not loop.

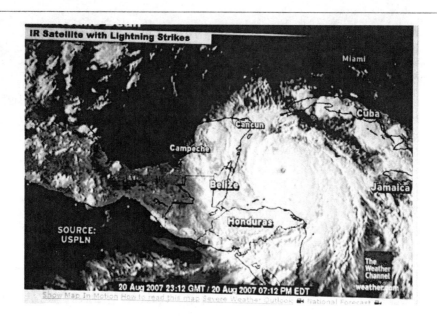

This enhanced satellite picture clearly shows the eye of Hurricane Dean as it moves across Central America.

So next time you're trying to decide whether to call a crew together for a flight a week away and don't want to be surprised by weather check the satellites to see if anything is headed your way!

Standard Weather Briefing - Part 5

Forecast Conditions
The Area Forecast (FA)

If you mention the San Joaquin valley, most people know it is in California, but do they know that it will be covered with a thick blanket of fog when the rest of the state boasts clear skies? You may know that the continental divide is in the Rocky Mountains, but how does it affect the weather in the region? Where is the hill country of Texas? Who cares?

Meteorologists care. Those hills create a barrier to onshore winds carrying moisture inland from the gulf. In stable conditions this means low fog that can last well into the morning across a third of the state. In unstable weather they provide an initial lift factor for afternoon summer thunderstorms.

Many pilots do not bother to study the area forecasts, preferring to look primarily at METAR's and TAF's, or Terminal Forecasts to determine enroute weather. All forecasts are the predictions of the development and/or movement of weather phenomena based on meteorological observations and various mathematical models. Area Forecasts give a general synopsis of atmospheric conditions affecting the flight and the macroclimatic effects this causes over various locations and terrains.

The difference is that TAF's are like knowing that pushing the stick forward makes you descend. Area Forecasts are like knowing why you descend. Long term acquaintance with the Area Forecasts allow a deeper understanding of how a weather system moving over local terrain affects the region.

One difficulty for those flying in a new area is not knowing the terrain landmarks the NWS is referring to. Attached is the map used by the NWS and ATC which delineates how area forecast data is applied.

Area Forecasts also separate their forecasts by states and parts of states. Texas is split into six basic parts which are further defined by the terrain within those areas. Though Massachusetts is much smaller, the state has three distinctive weather pattern areas.

Using the map on the opposite page and looking at the area forecast a little each day will allow you to grow into a deeper understanding of how various weather phenomena will affect flight conditions in your area. You can easily find the daily area forecasts on www.aviationweather.gov, the left hand bar will say TAF for Terminal Forecasts and FA for Area Forecasts.

(NOTE: As of this time the NWS is preparing to release graphical Area Forecasts to replace the written version. This is scheduled for early 2017)

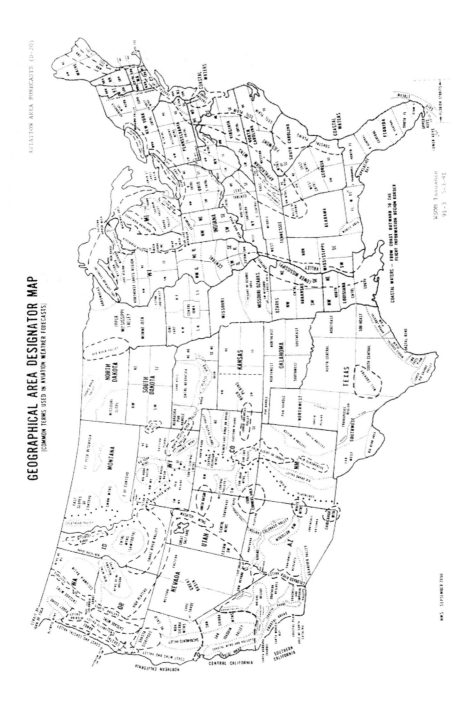

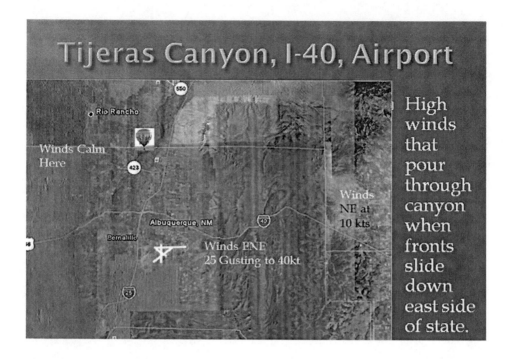

A Terminal Forecast (TAF) is a forecast of weather valid for a 5 mile radius of a single airport. In the picture above Albuquerque International Airport will have very strong surface winds whenever a low pressure system slides down the east side of Tijeras Canyon, while at the same time the launch point of the International Balloon Fiesta, only 12 miles to the northwest frequently has calm wind conditions.

Terminal Forecast (TAF)

One of the easiest forecasts to read can be also one of the most deceptive when it comes to predicting what the weather enroute or at the destination might be. A terminal forecast is just that, a forecast provided by the National Weather Service that is supposed to indicate what the weather will be like at that specific airport.

Even though the data is supposed to be used only for a five statute mile radius of a specific airport, many people use them as indications of condition at other airports within 20 or even 30 miles. Some people even use them in preference to the area forecast to determine enroute conditions.

A TAF, or terminal forecast, has advantages that an area forecast does not. The most popular of which is that it separates weather phenomena by specific time periods. We like specific information whenever possible, and pilots in particular want to know exactly when that snowstorm is going to hit the airport. The National Weather Service does a really great job overall of predicting the movement and timing of air masses, and NWS forecasters who have worked an area for a long time know how the terrain will affect incoming weather.

Some TAF's give hourly weather changes during times when rapid air mass movement is expected. Keep in mind that the NWS also states that TAF's can be off by an hour either direction, so don't expect that thunderstorm to hit at exactly 1532 Zulu!

To return to my previous statement, TAF's are seductive because you are tempted to think that a TAF issued at one airport may be gospel for another airport only ten or fifteen miles away. Double Eagle Airport (AEG) is twelve miles west of Albuquerque International (ABQ). AEG does not have a TAF, neither does Los Lunas (E80) 15 miles south, or Moriarty (0E0) 25 miles east. Because it is the only TAF within 50 miles of these airports, it is logical to look at it just to get a feel for what's going on, but local pilots know that when the wind is out of the east the conditions at ABQ are dramatically different from all those other airports because an east wind funnels through Tijeras Canyon directly at Albuquerque's main east-west runway. The other airports may not even have a five knot breeze.

ABQ also sits on the west side of Manzano Mountain, where Moriarty (0E0) is on the east side. 0E0 can have a two foot snowfall while ABQ barely gets a dusting. Also, keep in mind that while Area Forecasts are in mean sea level (MSL), TAFs are written specifically in AGL altitudes. The cloud heights will be very different in higher terrain. An Area Forecast will read ten thousand overcast for a large mountainous area-which could mean mountain obscuration, a TAF in that area might say three thousand overcast. This is confusing until you realize the surface of the airport is at seven thousand feet elevation.

A TAF is issued after the NWS receives at least two hours worth of current conditions reported at specific airports. Most of these airports have AWOS or ASOS stations that automatically report twenty four hours, but some still have humans inputting the data, so those that do not report at night, or if the automated weather station is down, will not get a TAF. TAF's must be issued for any airport that wishes to have commercial traffic.

TAFs are issued four times a day. In Zulu these times are 0000z, 0600z, 1200z, and 1800z. Most of them are for a twenty four hour period. Larger airport TAFs can go out for thirty six hours. All cloud covers are either SKC for sky clear, SCT for scattered, BKN broken and OVC overcast. BKN and OVC are considered "ceilings" and these are the only layers that determine MVFR or IFR classification. The numbers next to the cloud cover are in thousands of feet – so automatically add two zeros to the end of the number. (150BKN = 15,000 broken Weather phenomena are coded, RA for Rain, -RA for light rain, BR for Mist - which is a light fog – FG is fog, but is only used when it causes visibility to go below 1 mile. A complete list of weather contractions can be found at in the AC-0045 NWS guide to aviation weather.

Let's look at a couple TAFs and their interpretation.

KABQ 211134Z 2112/2212 VRB03KT P6SM OVC150 FM211900 23007KT P6SM SCT070 BKN130 FM220200 35005KT P6SM BKN035 OVC080

At KABQ (Albuquerque) this TAF covers the period on the 21st from 1200 zulu to the 22nd at 1200 zulu. Beginning at 1200z to 1900z the winds are expected to be variable at 3 knots, visibility is 6 miles or more (read P6SM as Plus 6 statute miles). Cloud cover is expected to be overcast at 15,000 feet AGL, good VFR weather. Sometime around 1900z (1 pm Mountain Daylight Time or 2pm Mountain Standard time), a lower scattered layer at 7000 feet will move in and the ceiling will lower to 13,000. By 0200z –in the evening— the ceiling goes down to 3,500 broken – close to marginal VFR and considering Albuquerque's altitude, probably a time when mountain obscuration will become a factor.

Here is a more specific forecast for San Diego, California, written for a thirty six hour time period.

KSAN 211608Z 2116/2218 VRB04KT 1SM RA BR FEW006
OVC023
> *TEMPO 2116/2118 2SM -RA BR OVC015*
> *FM211800 16010G20KT 3SM RA BR SCT010 OVC020*
> *FM220200 25010KT 4SM BR VCSH OVC015*
> *FM220800 16010G20KT 2SM +RA BR OVC005*
> *FM221600 18010KT 4SM BR BKN020CB*

At the time of the forecast issuance for two hours they expect IFR conditions – visibility only 1 mile in moderate Rain and Mist. A few clouds at 6 hundred feet with an overcast at two thousand three hundred. Although the overcast is Marginal VFR (MVFR), the visibility is IFR and only one has to have that criteria for the airport to be considered IFR. The word TEMPO means temporarily or occasionally, so during that first two hours the NWS feels that occasionally the visibilities could go up to two miles, and the ceilings could lower to one thousand five hundred. This makes a difference to some aircraft with varying landing minimum requirements.

At about 1800z there is expected to be a significant difference. IFR conditions will improve to MVFR overall, but the wind speeds will pick up becoming south-southeasterly at ten gusting to 20 knots. At 1600z we see that the cloud cover is BKN020CB. If there is a code such as CB appended to the cloud cover altitude it describes the kind of clouds, in this case CB means cumulonimbus – so thunderstorms could be moving in.

TAFs are very useful tools, indispensible to safe flight. Use them, but keep in mind their limitations!

NOTE: TAFs for military installations are written according to ICAO standards and use Meters instead of miles.

Standard Weather Briefing ‑ Part 6
Winds Aloft Forecast (FD)

"Every Way the Wind Blows"

I stand in a delightfully calm garden and watch as the clouds rip briskly only a few hundred feet above my head. Even more amazing is that at a higher level I can see mare's tail cirrus blowing in a completely different direction.

Winds can make a pilot's trip quicker or slower; a gentle lovely flowing drift or a nasty washboard gut wrenching misery. Pilots who research the winds aloft forecast can prepare themselves and their passengers for whatever experiences await them as they fling themselves into the sky.

The National Weather Service releases high altitude balloons from sites across the country two hours before the winds aloft forecasts are modeled for dissemination. These balloons carry equipment to measure humidity levels and a tracking device which enables the meteorologist to read its direction and speed by computer as it climbs into the flight levels.

Once the data is received they use it plus what they can see on radar and satellite together to forecast what is happening aloft. The Winds Aloft data is released every 6 hours, 0200z, 0800z, 1400z, and 2000z. The forecast data goes out in 6, 12, and 24 hour increments, reflecting how the winds are expected change over the day.   Most aviation weather websites carry it, but the NWS website is: http://aviationweather.gov/products/nws/winds

The winds are in MSL, beginning at 3,000 feet. They are given every 3,000 feet to 12,000, thereafter they are every 6,000 feet. Wind forecasts are not issued for altitudes within 1,500 feet of a location's elevation.   For instance, Albuquerque sits at 5400 MSL, this is too low for the 6,000 foot forecast, so the first data given is for 9,000 feet.

Winds aloft data also contain temperatures. Temperature forecasts are not issued for altitudes within 2,500 feet of a location's elevation.

Wind direction is indicated in tens of degrees (two digits) with reference to true north and wind speed is given in knots (two digits).   Light and variable wind or wind speeds of less than 5 knots are expressed by 9900.

Forecast wind speeds of 100 through 199 knots are indicated by subtracting 100 from the speed and adding 50 to the coded direction. For example, a forecast of 250 degrees, 145 knots, is encoded as 7545. Forecast wind speeds of 200 knots or greater are indicated as a forecast speed of 199 knots. For example, 7799 is decoded as 270 degrees at 199 knots or greater.

Temperature is indicated in degrees Celsius (two digits) and is preceded by the appropriate algebraic sign for the levels from 6,000 through 24,000 feet. Above 24,000 feet, the sign is omitted since temperatures are always negative at those altitudes. An example of this is seen below

DATA BASED ON 010000Z
VALID 010600Z FOR USE 0500-0900Z.

FT	3000	6000	9000	12000	18000	24000	30000	34000	39000
MKC	9900	1709+06	2018+00	2130-06	2242-18	2361-30	247242	258848	550252

The Kansas City (MKC) winds data is based on computer forecasts generated the first day of the month at 0000 UTC.   It is valid for use from 0500 UTC to 0900 UTC. Since MKC is only 757 feet MSL, the first wind data is forecast at 3,000 feet where the 9900 indicates that the winds are light and variable.

At 6,000 feet the winds are from 170 degrees (south) at 9 knots. By 9,000 feet they become a bit more westerly at eighteen knots, and by twelve thousand they are south-southwest (210 degrees) at thirty knots. Notice that at 6,000 feet there is a plus sign and the numbers 06. This means the temperature at that altitude is expected to be plus 6 degrees celcius. By 9,000 feet the temperature is zero – indicating where the freezing level is expected to be. Above 24,000 feet the temperatures are all expected to be negative, so they drop the plus/minus signs.

Notice the 39,000 foot winds. Forecast wind speeds of 100 through 199 knots are indicated by subtracting 100 from the speed and adding 50 to the coded direction. For example, a forecast of 250 degrees, 145 knots, is encoded as **7545**.

Since the direction at FL390 is over 360 degrees –in order to correctly interpret the data you must subtract 50 from the direction and add 100 to the speed. So the winds are actually 250 degrees at 102 knots, temperature minus 52 degrees celcius.

Some, not all, stations carry winds aloft temperatures up to 53,000 feet. These are usually shown on a separate line as seen below.

DATA BASED ON 091200Z
VALID 091800Z FOR USE 1400-2100Z. TEMPS NEG ABV 24000

FT	3000	6000	9000	12000	18000	24000	30000	34000	39000
ABI		1931+10	1929+10	2024+06	2331-10	2448-23	235239	246348	256056
ABQ			2213+03	2327-04	3163-17	3366-27	337242	326946	335749
ABR	2017	2312+14	2308+09	2615+02	2724-13	2527-26	273641	274051	274562

FT	45000	53000
ABI	301049	281149
ABQ	235061	244859
ABR	224559	243756

The winds on the previous page are for Abilene, TX, Albuquerque, NM and Aberdeen, SD. Note how Aberdeen's winds begin at 3,000, but the winds for Abilene and Albuquerque begin higher due to their surface altitude. One of my favorite pilot blunders is when a rookie on his first trip from the plains into the mountains asks me for the winds at 3,000 over Albuquerque. That's when I ask where he got the drill added to his propeller.

Look at the ABQ winds between 12,000 and 18,000 – there is an 80 degree switch in direction and more than thirty knots of speed change – looks like an indicator of windshear and possible turbulence between those altitudes to me!

When scanning the winds aloft forecast watch for directional and speed changes between altitudes and between sites along your route. If you are traveling from Bangor, Maine (BGR) to Cincinnati, OH (CVG) the winds could look like this:

FT	3000	6000	9000	12000
CAR	3520	3123-6	2833-09	2836-15
BUF	0307	3110-8	2622-11	2628-15
AGC	9900	2506-04	2516-07	2527-12
CLE	1808	9900-05	2515-10	2629-16
CMH	1413	2305-02	2517-07	2525-14
CVG	1420	2010+00	2414-06	2626-10

Notice that there is a strong northerly wind at three and six thousand on departure but by nine thousand the winds are out of the west southwest for the entirety of the flight.

They reduce in speed and change direction by Alleghany in western New York and by Cleveland they are out of the south-southeast. The changes in speed and direction indicate that you've either crossed a front or over a longer distance you've left an area dominated by one surface low pressure and entered another one. At the higher altitudes the wind direction does not change as much and the speeds (and temperatures) are more consistant, so this is mostly a surface based system.

For fun sometime, look at the forecast winds aloft along a route before you look at any other weather product and see if you can visualize changes in the weather patterns – then look at the surface analysis and/or jet stream charts. You may surprise yourself at how much it can tell you!

The next section deals with another wind forecast product that is more detailed and handier if you are staying low and only going short distances.

RUC Wind Forecasts

Hang-gliders, balloonists, parachutists, sport pilots, pipeline pilots and others who travel at low altitudes in a given area may want to investigate a weather product recently developed by NOAA: Rapid Update Cycle (RUC) wind forecasts. This product was designed to serve users needing frequently updated short-range wind forecasts.

Winds aloft forecast data (FD) currently used by pilots and weather briefers during a preflight briefing present the wind forecast in time periods of several hours each through a 24-hour period and in 3,000 foot altitude increments.

The Rapid Update Cycle, (RUC) wind data is measured in 100 to 300 foot increments, hourly for up to a 12 hour period from the surface to around 14,000 feet. The data the RUC winds are based on comes from the same NEXRAD radar sources as the Velocity Azimuth Display (VAD) winds, combined with other synoptic forecast models.

The usefulness of this tightly compacted forecast model to sport pilots is obvious. Balloonists in competition are at the mercy of the winds and must frequently which is the best site to launch from to drift towards the competition area. The smallest variation in wind can determine if they will grab a key from a tall pole and win a new car or emulate Maxwell Smart-"I was *this* close…"

KNOW BEFORE YOU GO → WWW.PILOTSANDWEATHER.COM

RUC2 Data Analysis - ABQ   Page loaded on: Sun Nov 8 15:31:05 2009

Data presented is 9.9 nm @ 117 degrees from 35.0400000,-106.6083330: ABQ

View Flight Projection At various levels and forecast time in Google Earth.   RUC

Forecast Time		Nov 08 2009 14:00Z	Nov 08 2009 15:00Z	Nov 08 2009 16:00Z	Nov 08 2009 17:00Z	Nov 08 2009 18:00Z	Nov 08 2009 19:00Z	Nov 08 2009 20:00Z	Nov 08 2009 21:00Z	Nov 08 2009 22:00Z	Nov 08 2009 23:00Z	Nov 09 2009 00:00
MSL (ft)	AGL (ft)	Direction & Speed	Direction & Speed	Direction & Speed	Direction & Speed	Direction & Speed	Direction & Speed	Direction & Speed	Direction & Speed	Direction & Speed	Direction & Speed	Direction & Speed
6516	0	87 @ 5	85 @ 3	130 @ 0	298 @ 3	293 @ 4	281 @ 6	288 @ 5	295 @ 4	279 @ 3	254 @	241 @
6568	52	116 @ 5	102 @ 4	220 @ 0	302 @ 3	294 @ 4	284 @ 6	288 @ 6	297 @ 5	281 @ 4	255 @ 4	249 @
6673	157	233 @ 7	247 @ 4	279 @ 1	303 @ 3	297 @ 4	284 @ 7	290 @ 6	298 @ 5	282 @ 4	257 @ 4	253 @
6831	314	258 @ 6	286 @ 5	305 @ 3	308 @ 4	301 @ 5	287 @ 7	293 @ 7	302 @ 6	285 @ 5	257 @	253 @
7041	524	276 @ 8	295 @ 9	316 @ 8	315 @ 5	307 @ 5	290 @ 7	294 @ 7	303 @ 6	287 @ 5	260 @	255 @
7362	846	287 @ 12	303 @ 14	323 @ 14	329 @ 8	316 @ 5	297 @ 7	299 @ 7	306 @ 6	289 @ 5	263 @ 6	260 @
7684	1168	291 @ 14	303 @ 17	318 @ 17	330 @ 14	331 @ 6	306 @ 7	304 @ 7	310 @ 6	291 @ 5	265 @ 5	262 @
8008	1492	292 @ 16	302 @ 19	316 @ 19	325 @ 16	341 @ 8	315 @ 8	310 @ 8	314 @ 6	295 @ 5	270 @ 5	271 @
8337	1820	296 @ 18	301 @ 20	312 @ 20	320 @ 17	339 @ 13	322 @ 10	315 @ 9	317 @ 7	298 @ 5	275 @ 5	279 @
8668	2152	294 @ 19	299 @ 21	309 @ 21	315 @ 18	331 @ 14	324 @ 12	318 @ 10	319 @ 7	300 @ 6	279 @ 5	293 @
8999	2483	294 @ 19	298 @ 22	306 @ 22	311 @ 19	325 @ 15	322 @ 14	318 @ 10	320 @ 7	302 @ 6	286 @ 5	306 @
9337	2821	294 @ 19	295 @ 22	303 @ 22	307 @ 19	320 @ 15	317 @ 15	316 @ 11	319 @ 8	302 @ 7	289 @ 6	313 @
9678	3162	296 @ 19	293 @ 22	300 @ 22	303 @ 19	314 @ 15	311 @ 15	309 @ 13	312 @ 9	302 @ 8	292 @	317 @
10020	3504	295 @ 19	291 @ 22	298 @ 22	299 @ 19	308 @ 14	303 @ 15	298 @ 13	301 @ 10	298 @ 9	295 @	317 @
10236	3720	293 @ 20	290 @ 23	297 @ 22	297 @ 19	304 @ 14	298 @ 15	294 @ 14	295 @ 11	295 @ 10	295 @ 10	316 @
10367	3851	292 @ 21	289 @ 23	296 @ 22	296 @ 19	302 @ 14	295 @ 15	291 @ 14	292 @ 12	292 @ 11	295 @ 10	315 @
10715	4199	290 @ 22	288 @ 23	294 @ 22	293 @ 19	294 @ 14	288 @ 15	285 @ 15	284 @ 13	285 @ 13	294 @ 12	313 @
11070	4554	289 @ 23	288 @ 24	293 @ 22	290 @ 19	287 @ 14	281 @ 15	278 @ 16	274 @ 15	260 @ 14	292 @ 1	309 @ 10
11424	4908	290 @ 24	288 @ 24	291 @ 22	286 @ 20	281 @ 15	275 @ 17	271 @ 17	267 @ 16	278 @ 15	290 @ 14	305 @ 11
11785	5269	290 @ 24	288 @ 24	290 @ 22	284 @ 21	276 @ 16	269 @ 18	264 @ 19	262 @ 17	275 @ 16	289 @ 15	303 @ 12

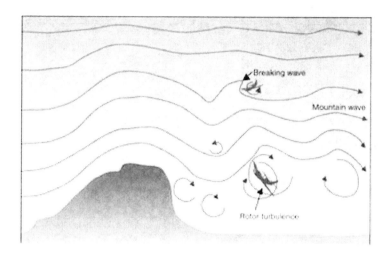

Breaking wave

Mountain wave

Rotor turbulence

Wild and Wicked Wind Shear

The sky is clear, the temperatures are comfortable at altitude, you can see a hundred miles in every direction. You've even been enjoying a bit of a tailwind. Suddenly, as though a couple of F15's had buzzed by, your flight takes on a new dimension in the struggle to be straight and level. Up becomes down, your seat belts barely restrain you from connecting with the ceiling and bolts creak as the fuselage metal stresses against opposing forces. This is wind shear.

According to Webster's definition, wind shear is a difference in wind speed and direction over a relatively short distance in the atmosphere. Wind shear can be broken down into vertical and horizontal components. Horizontal wind shear is primarily seen across weather fronts and near the coast. Vertical shear typically occurs near the surface, though it can also be generated at jet stream altitudes and near the tops of strong upper level fronts. A combination of both occurs during microburst activity wherein a strong downdraft hits the earth's surface and spreads out laterally.

The National Weather Service (NWS) categorizes wind shear by speed and direction. Shear speed is the component of wind shear which is due to a change in wind speed with height, e.g., southwesterly winds of 20 mph at 6,000 feet increasing to 50 mph by 12,000 feet. Speed shear is an important factor in severe weather development, especially in the middle and upper levels of the atmosphere.

http://www.srh.noaa.gov/jetstream/tstorms/windshear.htm

Directional shear is the component of wind shear which is due to a change in wind direction with height, for example southeasterly winds at the surface and southwesterly winds aloft. A wind which veers dramatically with height in the lower part of the atmosphere is a type of directional shear often considered important for tornado development. We see this during those hot summer months when tornadoes rip through the plains.

The NWS keeps a close eye on charts and weather conditions in order to provide pilots with accurate forecasts through Terminal Aviation Forecasts (TAF). If wind shear is anticipated it is encoded with "WS" and always follows the forecast surface winds.

If the airport surface winds are forecast to be 14012KT and a thunderstorm is in the area, you may see "VRB45KT" included. This may be encoded as OCNL.

If the same forecast shows a possible wind shear zone at 1,500 feet in which the wind will change to 240 degrees at 20 knots, then it would be encoded in a TAF as "WS015/24020KT". The wind shear group would immediately follow the surface wind group, thus providing a clear indication of how dramatic the wind change (shear) is expected to be. If it is uncertain as to what the wind direction and speed might be above the shear zone, or the height itself is in question, then the group may only include "WS015" or "WS", respectively.

Wind shear may not always be specifically forecasted at an airport by the NWS, but the TAF, Area Forecasts and Radars may indicate that thunderstorms are expected. Thunderstorms are assumed to contain strong gusty winds, both surface and aloft, as well as sudden downdrafts and vertical wind shear.

Though wind itself cannot be seen, you can see the effects of wind shear by observing formations of clouds or by debris bouncing around the airport. Shear experienced during landing or climb out can be attributed to wind deflected from hangars and other buildings, terrain features such as hills and trees along the runway or from the vortices of other aircraft (wake turbulence).

Rotor clouds and standing lenticular cloud formations are visual indications of areas of strong windshear activity aloft. Rotor clouds appear to be long horizontal fluffy cotton balls at low to mid altitudes. They appear to be rotating slowly, but what you see are the outside edges. Inside the winds are much stronger.

Standing lenticulars clouds are also seen primarily at mid and higher altitudes, but they appear to have a long smooth cigar shape, or can appear saucer shaped like the classic UFO. These are encoded in METAR's as either ACSL (Alto Cumulus Standing Lenticulars) or CCSL (Cirro Cumulus

Standing Lenticulars). Frequently both the Rotor clouds and the lenticulars will form on the lee side of mountains. If you seen them, you may want to avoid flying into or near to them as they contain rapidly rotating horizontal tunnels of air.

Winds Aloft Forecasts or FD's are good indicators of expected wind shear. Recently I briefed a pilot at Double Eagle Airport in Albuquerque. He told me the winds at the airport were very light, and the nearby TAF at ABQ also indicated surface winds were expected to be light, but the ABQ FD indicated winds of 230045kt at 9,000 – which is only about 3,500 AGL. Using the VAD wind readouts I was able to confirm this condition. You see this condition frequently in southern California during the Santa Ana windflow.

The FD may also predict winds to be relatively light at two succeeding forecast altitudes, but the direction may be as much as 180 degrees different! For example, the FL060 winds are forecast to be 09015 (east at 15 knots), while the FL090 winds are forecast as 27015 (west at 15 knots). The shearing effect on your aircraft will happen somewhere between the two altitudes, sometimes in as small as 500 feet elevation.

One way of confirming wind shear is to check the VAD wind readout. The Vertical Azimuth Display (VAD) is a function available on some radar sites showing current winds at 1,000 foot increments above the surface. The data is updated every 6 minutes.

Pilot reports are always appreciated if you experience any wind shear. Low level wind shear (*wind shear within 2,000 feet of the surface*) is classified as an urgent pilot report if air speed fluctuates 10 knots or more or if the air speed fluctuation is unknown.

Low Level Wind Shear (LLWS) is entered as the first remark in the pilot report. LLWS may be reported as minus (-), plus (+) , or plus and/or minus

(+/-) depending on how it effects the aircraft. If your aircraft suddenly speeds up during landing, then just as you have compensated it just as suddenly slows or drags, this would be considered +/-.

Today's technology allows you to access a great deal of data concerning the potential for wind shear if you take the time to read and interpret the many products available. If you don't always do so – keep the barf bags well supplied.

ABQ AFSS 2001

Pilot Weather Briefing - Part 7

Notices to Airmen
Navigating the NOTAM Jungle

Towards the end of every Pilot Briefing, there comes a moment when the Briefer goes quiet, sometimes for just a few seconds, or maybe minutes, while he or she scans pages of Notices to Airmen to determine whether or not they apply to the upcoming flight.

There are several types of NOTAMS. Distant (D) NOTAMS are issued through Flight Service or input directly by airport managers, or others who have been authorized to input a specific type of NOTAM. The National Flight Data Center puts out the FDC NOTAMS, and the ARTCC's issue NOTAMS for Temporary Flight Restrictions (TFR), including the ever popular Domestic Event Network TFR's (also known as Presidential TFR's). All NOTAMs are available nationally to AFSS's, DUAT Vendors and other aviation websites.

D NOTAMs focus on things that may significantly affect your flight such as airport and Runway closures, Military Training Routes, Parachute Jumping and Restricted Area closures. They also include temporary changes to Instrument Approach/Departure procedures,   NAVAID and communications outages and Weather service Hi-Balloon Launches.

Unlighted radio towers, smokestacks, oil rigs, and windmills are also D

NOTAMS. It used to be that these obstruction light outages populated the NOTAM list to the point that any pilot planning to fly at 2000 AGL or higher must wade through hundreds of these NOTAMS to get to ones pertinent to their flight. This is part of the reason that the Pilot Briefers must slow down during the last section of the briefing. However, upgrades to the Flight Service briefing program allow the briefers to segregate these, decreasing the time to visually scan the list.

The TFR or Temporary Flight Restriction NOTAM is designed to create a sterile temporary airspace over a given area for a short period of time. To my knowledge the only exception to that rule are the ones over Disneyland and Disneyworld that have been in effect since 9/11. TFRs are issued by the Air Route Traffic Control Center (ARTCC) that controls that airspace. A TFR can be put into effect over areas of Forest Fire Fighting, large sporting events such as the Indianapolis 500, and aircraft accident investigations.

And then there is the VIP TFR. Even if you have briefed yourself and seen that the weather is perfect, PLEASE ensure that there are no VIP TFR's along your route, and if there are, then plot out whether they will affect your departure and destination airports. This is the type of TFR that is most violated and most likely to cause you to lose your license if it is violated.

When you plan any future flights you can access all the TFR information through WWW.TFR.FAA.GOV. The information is arranged by the city and state closest to the TFR and the type of TFR it is.

Pilots flying the east coast have become used to calling before every flight to see if a VIP TFR has been issued or changed. Pilots in other areas of the country are more at risk to miss one simply because they are rare west of the Mississippi. Some central and western pilots who are used to bopping out to the ramp, and jumping in the plane for a short hop have found themselves kissing pavement after being forced to land when they

132

inadvertently crossed the invisible line. So become very familiar with the requirements for flight around those areas.

The National Flight Data Center issues the NOTAMs that cover large events such as the Oshkosh Fly-in, the Daytona 500, and the Super Bowl. . Much of this information is printed and disseminated well in advance and published in the FAA's Notices to Airmen books. Some FDC's are issued that are not as well anticipated, such as procedures in affect for an incoming hurricane, or outages to GPS coverage. These FDC's are sent out to the AFSSs and other vendors to become part of a pilot brief.

The new National Security Information NOTAMs are issued via the FDC route. Most of these refer to procedures that have actually been in effect since 9/11. Unfortunately, after long periods of time, it is easy to forget that no one is allowed to fly close to power plants, military bases or stadiums full of people..

All NOTAMs are available to you through the AFSS or through online briefing programs The NOTAM formatting is designed so that computers can be programmed to pick up on the keywords and separate types of NOTAMs into categories.

These are the Keywords that the NOTAMs will contain:

AD	Airport (Aerodrome)
RWY	Runway
TWY	Taxiway
APRON	Aprons and Ramps
OBST	Obstruction (tower lights etc)
NAV	NAVAIDs
COM	Communications
SVC	Service (Tower, FBO, etc)
AIRSPACE	Anything that affects aircraft in flight.

AD is the new keyword for Airport NOTAMs instead of AP because it is the international contraction for Aerodrome, which can be an airport, a seaport or a heliport.

Here are a few examples:

ABQ 09/005 NAV CNX VOR OTS
ROW 10/030 SVC ROW TWR CLSD
SAF 09/004 SAF AD AP WIP SN REMOVAL

Eventually, if the computer can separate all the NOTAMS into these groups, then when you are being briefed, the Briefer will not bother to open up the pages full of unlighted radio towers during the day or whenever you are traveling well above that altitude. No one will need to sift through surface information for the hundred airports enroute just to find information that could be pertinent.. This should save the Briefers and the pilots a good deal of time.

Airport managers, airshow managers, pilots who do aerobatics and many other can legally issue NOTAMs, but be advised, ONLY airport managers can issue one on surface conditions at the airport. If you need to issue a NOTAM call 1-877-4-US-NTMS (1-877-487-6867). The voice system will ask what state you are calling about and send you directly to the person handling that state. You may be on hold if they are taking another call, but this way you will be assured of reaching the person who will be familiar with your area.

The Dreaded TFR

Temporary Flight Restriction NOTAMs, or TFRs are becoming the most dreaded portion of a pilot briefing. Frequently a pilot will call Flight Service and say that the only thing he wants to know is if there are any TFRs between his departure and his destination.

If that is the only thing you call for – GOOD! These days busting a TFR can get you either a heavy fine or a suspended license. Trust me, ATC will do all it can to make sure you know where not to fly.

TFRs can be issued to protect airspace over airshows, major sporting events, volcanoes, forest fires, aircraft accident sites or anywhere else it is deemed unwise for aircraft to fly either for their own protection, or for security reasons.

Any TFR restricts certain aircraft from flying within specific areas. These areas are defined both geographically and by altitude. For instance, a TFR that is issued for a forest fire may restrict all aircraft from flying within a 10 mile radius of a NAVAID, such as a VORTAC, or Latitude/Longitude (L/L) point or if the area is particularly large, a series of radial/DMEs or L/L points may be used to define it. The TFR will also contain an altitude from the surface upwards which may be defined as either MSL or AGL.. Aircraft must fly over it or around it.

The TFRs are issued according to specifications in the Code of Federal

Regulations. If you look it up, find 14 CFR. Each type of TFR relates to a different section of that document. Some of them have exceptions to the rule, as with a forest fire TFR where the pilot's home base is within the restricted area, but you have to thoroughly read the section of 14 CFR that is specified in the TFR to determine if it allows any exceptions.

A Presidential TFR, also known as a VIP TFR is more complicated and pilots in those areas are monitored intensely. It is issued several days in advance and effective throughout the Presidential visit.

Shortly after the events of September 11, 2001, the Secret Service requested larger TFRs, limiting the ability of aircraft to fly in any airspace over or near wherever the President happens to be. Prior to this time, if the President landed at any airport, no other aircraft were allowed to takeoff, land, or taxi until he physically departed the airport grounds, this is still the case. However, once he left, the airport's traffic flow returned to normal.

This is no longer true. Several days prior to a Presidential visit, the FAA issues a VIP Temporary Flight Restriction (TFR) which is transmitted to all Air Traffic Control facilities and online to those websites that serve the aviation community. The TFR describes concentric circles around wherever the President is planning to be. Typically, the outer circle may be a radius from 10 to 30 miles wherein all aircraft flying below 18,000 feet must be in contact with Air Traffic Control and identified on radar. Aircraft can still land and depart from airports located in that area. You must be on a VFR or IFR flight plan, and a transponder code is required.

The inner circle is usually a 10 mile radius wherein only specific aircraft are allowed to fly at all, usually military, police and emergency medical flights, and scheduled air carriers . The bad part about this is that any airports that exist within that 10 mile radius cannot have any activity at all for the duration of the TFR, which can be from a few hours to several days.

This means no landings and no departures by civilian aircraft, with the exception of those involved in emergency operations and law enforcement.

In other words, if you are flying on an airline, your landing or departure will be delayed while the president is physically at the airport, but once he leaves you will be allowed to continue. However, say you wanted to hop into your private plane and get your currency, or fly up to Aunt Mabel's place, until the TFR is lifted you will not be allowed to leave or arrive at that airport – or any other airport within the 10 mile boundary. This also applies to part 135 air taxis and package haulers.

For example, let us assume Air Force One were to land at Phoenix International, and then the President was driven to a hotel 5 miles east where he was to stay during the course of his visit. For whatever length of time he was there, no unauthorized aircraft would be allowed to land or depart from the airports located at Mesa, Stellar, Williams or Chandler airports, as well as Phoenix itself.

Many times the fact that the President is planning a visit to a community is published in the local newspapers even before a TFR is issued as the TFR may only come out a few days in advance. TFR's are also issued for the Vice-President, but they are smaller, usually a 3 NMR below 3,000 AGL.

If you are planning any future flights you can access all the TFR information throughWWW.TFR.FAA.GOV. The information is arranged by the city and state closest to the TFR and the type of TFR it is.

Presidential TFRs are listed under VIP. If you click on a listing, the computer will bring up a map and dialogue concerning when and where pilots are not allowed to fly. If you access the list, you can limit the list by clicking on TYPE and then selecting VIP from the dropdown list. Under the map there is a link called "sectional chart" which shows the boundaries in more detail including what airports will be affected. The information concerning Time periods in a Presidential TFR are written in both Universal Coordinated Time (UTC) and in local time using a 24 hour clock

All TFRs are an inconvenience, but a necessary one. If you look outside and it is a beautiful day to fly, we still encourage you to call Flight Service for a brief, even if your only question is "Are There any TFRs today?"

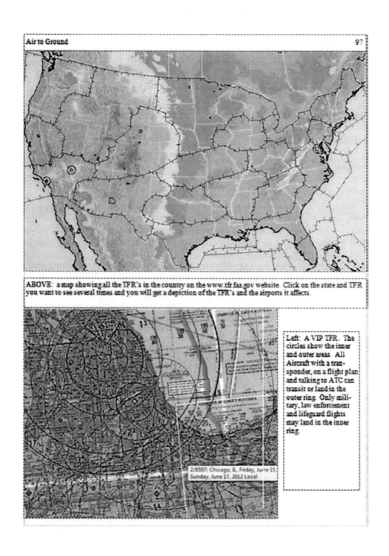

ABOVE: a map showing all the TFR's in the country on the www.tfr.faa.gov website. Click on the state and TFR you want to see several times and you will get a depiction of the TFR's and the airports it affects.

Left: A VIP TFR. The circles show the inner and outer areas. All Aircraft with a transponder, on a flight plan and talking to ATC can transit or land in the outer ring. Only military, law enforcement and lifeguard flights may land in the inner ring.

2/8597: Chicago, IL, Friday, June 15, Sunday, June 17, 2012 Local

FICON NOTAMs
Ramping Up for Winter

The leaves are turning red and gold as the season slides slowly into winter. It's time to brush up on all those things pilots need to know and do related to cold weather flying. De-icing techniques, ways to avoid areas the NWS has identified in AIRMETs as being likely to cause icing, and Field Condition (FICON) NOTAMs at airports.

FICONs identify any contaminant that affects landing and taxing surfaces at an airport. In addition to snow, ice, and water, these can refer to mud, ash, oil, sand and rubber buildups. This article focuses on those contaminants related to weather. During winter weather events, airports catering to commercial flights are required to update the FICON information on runways, taxiways and aprons/ramps frequently – at least once every 24 hours.

All public use airports are encouraged to update their FICON NOTAMs often as well. However there are small, remote airports up in the mountains who wait for the first big snowfall, then the manager – usually a government official who works 60 miles away, issues a NOTAM stating the airport has three feet of snow on the runway from now until next May, and another one that states "Conditions Not Reported" until that time.

A "Conditions Not Monitored" FICON NOTAM is issued in connection with a specific surface – such as a runway, indicated that no one will be updating the information for that surface during that date/time period. A similar NOTAM can be issued as "Conditions not Reported" which covers the entire airport. This one is not a FICON since it does not relate to just one surface.

These NOTAMs frequently cover weekends at airports where the person who issues NOTAMs, usually the manager, is only on the field from Monday to Friday. If a pilot should land or visit airports while a "Conditions Not Monitored/Reported" NOTAM is active, they can call flight service and have a PILOT REPORTED FICON issued. Their observations concerning the surfaces will not remove the previous NOTAMs, but the information will appear for a period of up to 12 hours, or when the manager returns.

In the past, airport managers came up with a wide variety of descriptions for the types of ice and or snow that contaminate a surface. The U.S. NOTAM office has pared the list of allowable descriptions considerably.

There are 3 types of snow – wet, dry and compacted. You can also use Wet, Ice, slush and Water. Wet snow allows you to form a snowball, dry snow blows around and compacted snow must be chipped through. You cannot use any other description of the contaminant – such as rough, slick, frozen etc…

Depth is not reported when a surface is described as WET and the term DRY is only used when a surface is significantly different in one area versus another – for instance when the center portion of the runway is deiced and dry while the sides still have 2 inches of snow.

Depth is mandatory for runway NOTAMs containing DRY SN, WET SN, WATER or SLUSH. It is optional for taxiway or apron/ramp NOTAMs.

The depth is not allowed for ICE or COMPACTED SN, since they are both slick regardless of the depth, so it is not needed. The USNO does allow a NOTAM to indicate if there are other contaminants on top of ICE or COMPACTED SN, but those two cannot be one atop the other. WATER, SLUSH, DRY SN, or WET SN can be single layers or listed as top layers.

General aviation airport managers have been frustrated for years because they are not allowed to issue one set of conditions for the whole airport. FICONs can be issued for All Taxiways or All Aprons, but separate FICONs must be issued individually for runways.

You can have NOTAMs issued under the AD (Airport) keyword that will refer to what the airport is doing about surface conditions – such as AD ALL SFC WIP SN REMOVAL. (Translation: All surfaces on the airport are undergoing work-in-progress for snow removal.)

One last note, all FICON NOTAMs must have an observed at time so the pilot knows how long ago the condition was noted.

The Chart Supplements (formerly AFD's) will state the hours that airport management is on the field normally keeping all reports updated, but if for some reason they will be gone for an extended period of time outside those hours the managers may choose to issue a NOTAM for the whole airport.

AD AP CONDITIONS NOT REPORTED 1611032300-1611121300

If the conditions on a specific surface will not be reported for a length of time less than 24 hours, but that surface does have contaminants, the NOTAM may have multiple date/time groups.

TWY ALL 2IN DRY SNOW OBSERVED AT 1612251200. CONDITIONS NOT MONITORED 1612251230-1612261200. 1612251200-1612261200

In the NOTAM above, the first time is when the conditions on the taxiways were observed. Then it states that no one will update the conditions on the taxiways until the next morning. The final two sets of numbers state when the NOTAM went into effect and when it will expire.

Until October of 2016 the FICONs for taxiways, ramps, aprons and runways were formatted in a similar manner. In that year the format of runways NOTAMs changed. Here are some examples of taxiway and apron FICONs, the next section is devoted to runways.

TWY ALL 3IN WET SN OVER COMPACTED SN BA POOR 3FT SNOWBANKS OBSERVED AT 1609131400. 1609131400-1609141400

APRON MAIN RAMP WET ICE BA NIL OBSERVED AT 1609151400. 1609151400-1609161400

Runway FICON

What Do All Those Numbers Mean?

The heat of summer has not yet passed into icy memory, but with the fall we have to look forward to winter flying and more importantly…winter landings. With that in mind the FAA in has finally settled on a method to communicate to the flying public just how dangerous landing and takeoff conditions are when runways are compromised by weather related contamination.

For years now the FAA's NOTAM office has been tightening up all the NOTAMs so they are in compliance with ICAO standards. This has caused angst as the minutia associated with NOTAM formatting requirements has changed every year. The release of the next NOTAM handbook, JO 7930.2R in October of 2016 is nice in that overall there are very few differences from the last version – it's 95% the same. There is a small difference in how frequencies are presented (commas between each rather than solidus), and they have added the words "Slippery when wet" when describing runways with rubber accumulation.

The only major change is in the realm of FICONs (Field Condition NOTAMs) , and at that, you won't see any changes to how the FICONs on Taxiways and ramps look other than some new braking action terminology.

But the new formatting and data requirements for Runway field conditions is dramatically changed.

Why do they look so different?

In the past the way FICONs were issued was highly subjective as to the "slipperiness" of the surface. This lead to situations where pilots were unsure whether they could land and stop or slide all the way to the next town. The new system was devised by an international committee of airport managers, FAA, and aircraft manufacturers focused on how to develop a common understanding of what all the reported surface conditions mean to those who use the data to assess landing performance capabilities.

Where before you might see separate NOTAMs for braking action, Mu readings and runway surface contamination descriptions, the new system takes all those elements into account when creating a Runway Condition Code (RCC). In the past the NOTAMs have always referred to the full length of a runway. Now all runways are broken down into thirds during the assessment.

Airport managers are only supposed to issue these FICONs for the active runways, and only for one direction. The RCC code will consist of three numbers separated by solidus (ex: 3/4/5). Each number relates to the slipperiness level of the touchdown, midpoint, and rollout thirds of that runway. The RCC code levels are zero (absolutely no traction) through six (bone dry).

The RCC code numbers are only generated when at least 25% of the runway has some kind of contaminant. If there are only a few spots of snow, water, ice or whatever along the surface, the contaminants will be reported, but a code will not be generated.

Speaking of percentages, all the FICONs will now contain percentages within the NOTAM for each third of the runway along with the contaminants on that runway. The percentages reported by the airport managers are always rounded up. In the body of the FICON the thirds are separated by commas.

Let's look at one of these NOTAMs:

RWY 26 FICON 4/3/3 50 PRCT COMPACTED SN, 75 PRCT 1IN WET SN OVER COMPACTED SN, 90 PRCT 2IN WET SN OVER COMPACTED SN...

The RCC code is 4/3/3. The 4 is for the touchdown third which is described as having a 50% coverage of compacted snow. The second number is a 3. That is the slipperiness factor connected with the middle third or midpoint of the runway described here as 75% of that section having one inch of wet snow over the top of compacted snow.

The final number 3 means they have assigned the same slipperiness value to the rollout portion of the runway and it has 90% coverage of 2 inches of wet snow over compacted snow.

Notice that the descriptions of each third are separated by commas. In every case, if any of the thirds is different from the rest there will be comma separating the description of each third. If the surface of the runway is consistent in all thirds, the NOTAM may look like this:

RWY 30 FICON 5/5/5 100 PRCT WET DEICED LIQUID

Of course some of these FICONs will also contain information concerning plowed widths, deicing and snowbanks. Some of them may be appended with "Conditions Not Monitored" with the time periods attached.

One thing you will not see in this new system is an RCC code of zero. If the computer determines the conditions warrant a zero, it refuses to issue the NOTAM. Part 139 airports – ones where commercial traffic can land – are required to close any runway that has an RCC code of zero.

RCC codes are only generated for paved surfaces, so you won't see them on grass, dirt, or gravel runways. Those may still have FICONs that describe things in thirds, just no code up front.

Many small airports with short runways may opt to always present their information in a full length format like the one for Runway 30 above. You will not see braking action reports or mu values listed in the NOTAM – that data is used and fed into the computer to determine the RCC code.

If a runway is less than 25% contaminated, the NOTAM will show up without the RCC code. For instance, the first third has 50% coverage of slush, but the other two thirds are dry – so the total percentage for the whole runway comes to less than 25%. The NOTAM would look like this:

RWY 17 FICON 50 PRCT 1IN SLUSH, DRY, DRY

This shows that the full length of the runway has patchy areas of inch deep slush over 50% or less of the surface.

As I mentioned up front, the APRON and TWY FICONs will generally look the same as in the past. Airport managers can still put out separate braking action (BA) reports for them, though the terminology has changed. Instead of Poor, Fair and Nil, the terms to be used if there is any problems with braking are **good, good to medium, medium, medium to poor, poor.**

Although NIL is still a term used for braking action, Part 139 commercial airports are required to close any surface where this is reported instead of putting out a NOTAM. For that same reason RCC codes for Part 139 airports will never contain a zero (0).

You may still see a NIL report at general aviation airports. Many GA managers may decide to keep a surface open because they have no other options for helicopters or other activities.

Only the runways will be different. So as we fly into winter, be prepared to scrutinize the NOTAMs a bit until you are familiar with the relationship of the RCC codes to how far you'll slide down the runway yelling "WHOA, Big Fella!"

Information regarding these changes is available at:

http://www.faa.gov/about/initiatives/talpa

The FAA's governing document for all NOTAMs (Order 7930.2) is online. You can read it on the FAA website www.faa.gov, select the Air Traffic Tab, click on Air Traffic Plans and Publications.

**Parachuting, Hot Air Balloons and Blimps
may need to have a NOTAM issued!**

Do You Need to File a NOTAM?

As pilots you know what a Notice to Airmen (NOTAM) is, and the importance of looking them over prior to a flight. But have you ever had a need to issue one? Do you know when one is needed?

The only ones allowed to file NOTAMs for Airport surfaces are airport managers. Only FAA technicians can file them for communications outages or navigational aid outages. That leaves two areas where pilots or other civilians may file NOTAMs: AIRSPACE and OBST (Obstruction)

AIRSPACE NOTAMs include: Parachute Jumping, Aerobatics, Unmanned Rockets and Aircraft, Balloons, Airshows, Aerial Spraying, Controlled Burns, Hang Gliders, High Altitude balloons, Hot Air Balloon Rallies, Air Drops, Fireworks (aka PYROTECHNICS), Blasting, Aerial Refueling,

Some other, more unusual AIRSPACE NOTAMs have included Wire Walking (when the person is walking above 500 feet AGL), massive flights of small helium balloons and Chinese fire lantern releases. Basically, anything that may adversely affect the safe flight of manned aircraft must be NOTAMed.

Most airspace activities require a waiver to be issued by the FAA. To check and see if your activity will need a waiver, call the local Flight

Standards District Office in your area and talk with an agent. Be sure to begin this process at LEAST a month in advance. If a waiver is required it will state what kind of NOTAMs need to be issued.

Airspace NOTAMs require the following information:
1 latitude/longitude of the site in hours/minutes/seconds (NOT digital), or the radial/DME from the closest NAVAID, and/or the distance from the closest airport. If you don't know the last two we can find them based on the Latitude/Longitude.
2 The horizontal size of the activity. Do you need to protect a one mile radius, five miles? Or is the activity from point to point?
3 The Base and Height of the activity in Mean Sea Level
4 If based at the surface you can also add the Height above ground (AGL)
5 What time period will it cover? If it is for a portion of each day for successive days you can have one NOTAM that says something like Monday-Friday from sunrise to sunset, or 1200 to 2300 Greenwich Mean Time.
6. What day will it begin, what day will it end?

You can see the information encoded according to FAA/ICAO requirements here:

AIRSPACE AIRSHOW ACFT WI AN AREA DEFINED AS 5NM RADIUS OF EQY SFC-4000FT 1511061700-1511062200

AIRSPACE AEROBATIC AREA WI AN AREA DEFINED AS SGJ037002 TO SGJ347001 TO SGJ127001 TO POINT OF ORIGIN SFC-3500FT 1511211600-1511212000

AIRSPACE UAS WI AN AREA DEFINED AS 2NM RADIUS OF LOA199018 SFC-200FT AGL 1511241500-1511242300

NOTE:. There are literally thousands of unmanned air vehicles (drones or UAS) being sold in stores today. If they are non-commercial hobby aircraft – smaller than 55 pounds with a top altitude of 400 feet or less then they don't have to file a NOTAM as long as they stay over five miles away from an airport. They are supposed to stay away from any manned aircraft and obey privacy laws.

Drones flown for commercial or governmental purposes are supposed to file NOTAMs and have waivers.

The other type of NOTAM is OBST, or obstruction. Obstructions are cranes, moored balloons, oil rigs, wind turbines and tall radio towers. They can also be buildings, tall parked aircraft and on occasion hills.

The first question depends on several factors related to an OBST NOTAM is its location and its height above the ground. First, is it within 5 miles of any airport or helicopter routing? Will it be higher than 200 feet AGL? If the answer to both of those is no, then usually a NOTAM does not have to be issued, but you can do so if you want to.

If the answer to either is yes, then an Obstruction NOTAM needs to be issued. In order to do that correctly, you would call the phone number you called before and request to issue an Obstruction NOTAM.

The data the specialist needs for Obstruction NOTAMs is:

1. latitude/longitude of the site in hours/minutes/seconds (NOT digital)
2. The location reference the closest airport, or if it is on the airport, it's placement from a specified point on the airport, such as "500 FT West of the Approach end of RWY36."
3. The Base and Height of the activity in Mean Sea Level
4. The AGL height
5. It is lighted? Flagged?
6. What time period will it be a factor? Will it be there continuously? Or will it be something like a crane that is there for a portion of time each day for a week or a month?
7. What day will it begin, what day will it end?

The final NOTAM should end up looking something like this:

OBST MOORED BALLOON WI AN AREA DEFINED AS 1NM RADIUS OF 335849N1182524W (2NM S OF LAX) 340FT (200FT AGL) LGTD NOT FLAGGED DAILY SR-SS 1512131430-1512172359

One final note for both the OBST and AIRSPACE NOTAMs. If it is within 5 miles of an airport governed by an air traffic control tower, you will need to contact the Tower prior to setting it up and let them know what you intend to do. You are also required to contact the airport manager so he can advise the local pilots.

Photo by Dennis Livesay

Optional Briefing Items

In addition to all the items covered in a Standard Weather Briefing, Flight Service personnel have access to other data a pilot can request. These items are not required to be given so a pilot must ask for them specifically.

1. Special Use Airspace: MOA's, Military Training Routes (MTRs) Alert Areas and Warning Areas. (*Note: Non-published Restricted area NOTAMs must be given during a briefing.)
2. NOTAMs for Military Airports. If you are landing at a military airport be sure to request those NOTAMs separately. They are input by the military bases and show up in a different database than NOTAMs for civilian airports.
3. Density Altitude calculations
4. ATC delays into airports. (Including ground stops)
5. RAIM data
6. Runway Friction measuring NOTAMs. (These are frequently given though not required during a standard brief)
7. Special FDC instrument approach procedure changes.
8. Information connected with published NOTAMs about events such as Oshkosh, NASCAR races, the Super Bowl and Ski Area Airports — including reservation information.
9. Loran C NOTAMs
10. Other General Information (questions about air traffic services, frequencies, ADIZ rules, Search and Rescue, border crossing procedures

Chapter 13

Other Types of Briefings

Outlook Briefings

A pilot planning for long flights likes to get a feel for how weather will affect their plans well in advance. An Outlook briefing is given when a flight is more than six hours away. It contains all the sections of a standard brief related to forecast data, but is not required to contain current data including weather advisories, since six hours from now that data will not be pertinent. The Briefer can include current data if he feels it will help the pilot see trends in weather patterns.

Remember, for all types of briefings, Flight Service is required to make sure you are aware of any adverse conditions enroute. In an outlook briefing they won't give you specific weather service products such as convective SIGMETS but they will check forecasts for thunderstorm probabilities and they can look to see if any TFR's have been issued or if there is a NOTAM closing your destination airport.

Although many pilots call and say "look into your crystal ball" and ask for weather forecasts a week in the future, officially a Flight Service outlook briefing can only go out 48 hours – that's the extent of the official surface prognosis charts issued by the National Weather Service. Several commercial weather companies such as WSI have more generalized "prog" charts that extend up to 5 days and if you want data further than that you can look at the weather channel and see what their staff predicts. The further out you look, the less specific the data and the more room for error. These are graphics that forecast movements of fronts and air masses taking into account the energy and moisture content currently contained.

The printed weather products, such as Terminal Forecasts (TAF), Winds aloft, and area forecasts will not go beyond 24 hours in most cases, though some larger airports have TAF's which give forecast information up to 36 hours in advance.

Abbreviated Briefings

Abbreviated briefings are tricky. Pilots call and say they want an abbreviated brief, then they go quiet on us, as though we are expected to automatically become mind readers. An abbreviated brief means a pilot only wants one or two isolated pieces of information. You can simply ask for the NOTAMS at Wichita, or the winds from Dallas to Boston at FL240. If the Briefer gives you those winds, and then you ask for current and forecast conditions at Boston….They may launch into a standard brief format because you are now asking for more than just a couple of items.

The worst pilots to brief are ones that interrupt constantly and pick you to death. "Ohh, I only want this, and can you give me that, and what is it doing over here." As a briefer, I have to make sure that I have done everything I can to ensure you have all the information you need for a safe flight. The Standard Brief format is a checklist – just like the ones in your airplane. If I miss any item on that checklist that causes the pilot problems - I can have my certificate withdrawn and be out of a job. Do ask questions if the briefing was unclear, but please let the Briefer give you the data in standard order.

When a pilot lands on a closed runway and he has been briefed, investigations are done to see if there was a NOTAM about the closed runway at the time of the brief and if the NOTAM was given to the pilot. Was weather a factor? Did the specialist tell the pilot about the thunderstorms or the IFR conditions enroute? The creditability and dependability of Flight Service stems from the professionalism displayed by its specialists and the data they have at their fingertips.

Albuquerque National Weather Service Radiosonde Hi Altitude Balloon Launch Facility

Flying into Climate Change

The earth is warmer...or is it colder? The seasons are drier where it is usually wet and wetter where it is usually arid. Pacific islands are being swallowed by rising oceans created because the ice caps are melting. What has this got to do with flying?

Well, a lot actually.

Hundreds of pilots now have access to online weather services which give you all the data you are accustomed to seeing prior to a flight. But how many of you are reading it all? The Standard Brief that Flight Service developed decades ago still has current conditions and area forecasts, winds, NOTAMs and all those weather products that are the result of observations scoured from hundreds of stations across the world and floating above the earth. But like the meteorite in "Armageddon", most of us can't see what's coming until it is on top of us.

I spoke to a pilot briefer, Charles, recently who had briefed a Mooney pilot from Flagstaff, AZ to North Las Vegas, NV this morning. It was 5:30am and the pilot had pulled up all the usual data on the computer that you normally look for in a preflight briefing. He wasn't going to leave until 8am and come back in the afternoon, and being a little sleepy, he figured having a second opinion was not a bad idea. Charles had been on duty for an hour already and unlike the Mooney pilot he had looked not just at the current information but had pulled up the outlooks, the forecast lifted indexes and some crazy obscure data that all of us probably learned about in our NWS class, but don't use much.

What Charles remembered was that the Terminal Forecasts (TAF), Area Forecasts, and winds aloft all change between the time the Mooney pilot called and the time he wanted to leave. He had wanted to return to FLG in the latter part of the afternoon, and had figured it would be hot as usual and he'd have to compensate for density altitude, but the pilot had not realized that today was the day that the monsoon season would officially hit Arizona.

The briefer's assessment of thunderstorms developing and their pattern of movement was dead on. The Mooney pilot filed to VGT and made it there, but was forced to spend the night. Of course, being stuck in Vegas overnight is not really a bad thing.

All of us are accustomed to certain weather patterns in the regions in which we live and fly. But for the past few years weather patterns across the country are changing, becoming more dramatic. Flying requires us to be a part of the atmosphere. Taking a warm sunny day for granted can cause someone to be complacent. Talking to a professional briefer who is studying all the available NWS resources for eight hours a day can alert you to unusual changes. One reason is that he studies the outlooks and synopsis continuously.

How many of you know what a lifted index is? Glider pilots and balloonists check them all the time, but most private pilots don't. A lifted index indicates how likely a parcel of air is to move vertically given various other factors. Let's talk about stability.

A parcel of air can be:

> Unstable (Less than -5)
> Moderately Unstable (-1 to -5)
> Neutral (0)
> Moderately Stable (1 to 5)
> Stable (greater than 5)

The lifted index (LI) is a common measure of atmospheric stability. The Lifted Index Analysis Chart depicts a number associated with the stability of a surface parcel of air lifted to 500 mb. Lifted index values range from positive to negative. A positive lifted index indicates stable air. Larger positive numbers imply greater stability. A negative lifted index indicates unstable air. Larger negative numbers imply greater instability. A zero lifted index indicates neutrally stable air.

Say the day dawns bright, clear and cool, perfect for flying right? The Lifted Index shows a -5. This indicates that the atmosphere is marginally unstable. All it takes is a small change to begin uplift. Uplift means turbulence and if enough moisture is present, thunderstorms. By 10AM in the southwest the sun has heated the air to the point that lifting has begun. Though there is no front or trough, thunderstorms will develop as the somewhat humid airmass rises along the mountain slopes into the colder upper atmosphere.

That is the key to knowing when the monsoon season will hit the southwest. If you see a low pressure parked over the Baja, and a high over the Gulf of Mexico it means that ambient moisture is floating into Arizona and New Mexico. When the lifted index is negative, you can bet that afternoon heating will push the air upwards creating clouds first over mountain peaks. The storms will then drift whichever way the upper winds are blowing that day — which is why they are hit and miss.

Is climate change caused by people or is nature just doing what it has always done on its own?   Just because we can measure atmospheric changedoesn't mean we know all there is to know. I don't have the answer, but I do know that if you are going flying, it is best to have the most comprehensive knowledge possible of the environment which will surround you and your loved ones.   If you don't want to take the time to delve into the deeper parts of NWS charts and forecasts, then I suggest you call someone who does it for a living before you fly off for a weekend vacation.

A Final Note on Flight Service
Preflight Briefers

On September 11, 2001 shortly after the terrorist attacks on the American East Coast, the FAA grounded all aircraft throughout the United States. Most stayed grounded for days or weeks keeping everyone from general aviation to air carriers routed in place while the military figured out what was going on. During this time the pilots throughout the nation wanted to be kept informed—some of them were far from home. Who did they call?

Flight Service

The pilot weather briefing line is the only access individual pilots have to the latest information disseminated by the FAA. Pilots are comfortable talking to briefers as they do every day and whenever they have questions about practically anything, 1-800-WX-BRIEF is the number they call.

Tower and Center operations don't publish their phone numbers, but Flight Service has direct lines to all of them so that is the route many aviation enthusiasts will use to communicate with other arms of ATC.

What other kinds of information requests does FSS get?

• Pilots will call to inquire about special flight rules for Border Crossing, the Grand Canyon, ski airports, and traffic management programs for events such as the Super Bowl.

• Students will call for practice flight plans, briefings and to ask questions about maps, procedures, or weather.

• If you need to get hold of the Flight Standards District Office and don't know which one covers your airport, you call Flight Service.

• Specialized information is available for balloonists and glider pilots—lifted indexes, K index etc...

• Because pilots know flight service have the most current weather, they will call us before a sporting event and ask questions about which way a storm cell is moving or what is the reading on the VAD winds.

• Some pilots also tell their friends to call us for things not related to aviation such as:

• Construction companies call to ask if any rain is forecast when they want to pour concrete.

• TV stations call for information about accidents—these calls are forwarded to the FAA information offices.

• People call when they see UFO's to ask what it is. (We give them the national UFO hotline phone number)

https   .1800wxbrief.com   SouthWest Writers

w   Favorites   Tools   Help

FlightService   1800wxbrief   Better

Home | Pilot Dashboard | Weather ▾ | Flight Planning & Briefing ▾ | Airports ▾ | UAS ▾ | Account ▾ | Links

Mon S

Featured Capabilities

ACAS – Adverse
Condition Alerting
Service

NGB - Next
Generation Briefings

SE-SAR -
Surveillance-Enhanced
Search and Rescue

EasyActivate™ and
EasyClose™

**ACAS - Adverse
Condition Alerting
Service**

Monitors flight plans after briefing and filings. Sends
pilots alerts for changes in adverse conditions.

Read More

Chapter 14

Adverse Condition Alerting Service

How many times have you gotten a weather briefing and headed out to the aircraft and an hour into the flight the weather changed in a way that had not been predicted during your briefing? Have you ever wished there was a way for Flight Service to notify you when things change? Well now there is.

Flight Service has created an Adverse Condition Alerting Service (ACAS) which fills in the gap between briefing and flight time. The ACAS continuously monitors weather conditions from the time your flight plan is filed until the time it is closed after the flight. Any time that new or modified adverse condition information is received from the weather service, ACAS sends an email or text message and during the flight the alerts can be delivered through cockpit satellite communications devices. Several vendor devices are now supported, with more being added.

The ACAS not only notifies pilots of Adverse Weather conditions, but it also generates alerts for Temporary Flight Restrictions (TFRs) and airport/runway closed/unsafe NOTAMs and urgent PIREPs along the filed route of flight. The alerts do not contain the entire text of the adverse condition, they merely advise what updates are available and recommend you call flight service for more information.

The alerts are tagged to your flight plan at Flight Service so that if a pilot calls in, the specialist has immediate access to whatever safety-critical information is needed. Alerts are only sent if the pilot has registered for the service. Registration is free, straightforward and is done on the Pilot Web Portal. https://lmfsweb.afss.com/Website

The Flight Service PilotWeb has a lot of other excellent features. Not only can you do self-briefing if you prefer using all the information that Flight Service has access to, you can file, activate and close VFR flight plans. You can file IFR flight plans and unlike other flight plan filing services, if after you've filed you need to change something on the flight plan you can call LM Flight Service and they will have all the information there. Other services do not transmit the IFR flight plan info to flight service at all, so changing anything once filed can be a chore.

The PilotWeb can be personalized so that your home base weather pops up first when you log on. The progressive briefing information will color code weather stations enroute so that you can see if they forecast to stay VFR, or may change to IFR during your flight with one glance.

If you wish, you can set up the website for your flight and call flight service – then use it to follow the briefer through every step of the briefing – a great training tool for student pilots!

U.S. DEPARTMENT OF TRANSPORTATION FEDERAL AVIATION ADMINISTRATION **FLIGHT PLAN**	(FAA USE ONLY)	☐ PILOT BRIEFING ☐ VNR ☐ STOPOVER		TIME STARTED	SPECIALIST INITIALS

1 TYPE	2 AIRCRAFT IDENTIFICATION	3 AIRCRAFT TYPE/ SPECIAL EQUIPMENT	4 TRUE AIRSPEED	5 DEPARTURE POINT	6 DEPARTURE TIME		7 CRUISING ALTITUDE
VFR IFR DVFR			KTS		PROPOSED (Z)	ACTUAL (Z)	

8 ROUTE OF FLIGHT

9 DESTINATION (Name of airport and city)	10 EST. TIME ENROUTE HOURS MINUTES	11 REMARKS

12 FUEL ON BOARD HOURS MINUTES	13 ALTERNATE AIRPORT(S)	14 PILOT'S NAME, ADDRESS & TELEPHONE NUMBER & AIRCRAFT HOME BASE	15 NUMBER ABOARD
		17 DESTINATION CONTACT/TELEPHONE (OPTIONAL)	

16 COLOR OF AIRCRAFT	CIVIL AIRCRAFT PILOTS. FAR Part 91 requires you file an IFR flight plan to operate under instrument flight rules in controlled airspace. Failure to file could result in a civil penalty not to exceed $1,000 for each violation (Section 901 of the Federal Aviation Act of 1958, as amended). Filing of a VFR flight plan is recommended as a good operating practice. See also Part 99 for requirements concerning DVFR flight plans.

FAA Form 7233-1 (8-82)   CLOSE VFR FLIGHT PLAN WITH _____ FSS ON ARRIVAL

Chapter 15
Filing Your Flight Plan

You have a good idea as to where you are going and how to get there, now it is time to determine if you would like to file a flight plan. Flight plans are required for any aircraft flying by IFR rules. The data is input either through flight service, BASEOPS or a private vendor and sent to the appropriate ATC facility an hour prior to your proposed departure time. This enables the ATC computer to produce a data block of information overlaying the radar screens so the controllers can more easily track your flight and can look ahead to see if there may be any conflicts on the horizon.

Flight plans can also be filed for VFR aircraft. In many cases they are not required, but they are of great benefit to the pilot in many ways. Do you know where the idea of a VFR flight plan originated? With the military of course — during the War to end all Wars. In WWI aircraft were primarily used as scouts, finding the location of the enemy. The commanders told them to look over specific terrain and then report back. Then, as now, the squadron leaders scheduled where they were intending to fly and when they were expected to report back.

As both commercial and private pilots began entering the aviation arena procedures were put in place whereby search and rescue could be initiated should an aircraft become overdue. Responsibility for this action was given to the operators assigned to the Airway Radio Stations – forerunners of today's Flight Service. Over time the precise steps taken by Flight Service were designed so that if someone did find themselves landing prematurely, and managed to survive, trained search and rescue personnel would be looking for them within a short period of time. Statistics have shown that in such a circumstance the accident victim's chances of survival are highest when not exposed to the elements for over 24 hours.

As radar technology became available the ability to go IFR means that someone has their eye on you all the time, but as every pilot who has felt the thrill of leaping upwards into the air knows, it's more fun to just fly where you like rather than have someone always telling you where to go.

The VFR flight plan gives you that freedom and still offers the security of knowing someone will be searching for you if you do not arrive at your destination on time. There are other options of course. You could choose to have a family member or friends listen for you to call them when you land, but what if you land somewhere without cell phone coverage? How long should they wait beyond your ETA to raise an alarm? If they do have to raise an alarm have you instructed them on who to call and what information will be needed for Flight Service to start the SAR process? Do they know exactly what airport you left, what route you took and what your aircraft type and identification are?

If you can say with certainty that your support group is well trained in these matters and won't be distracted by a movie or participating in a local ballgame, then you probably don't need to bother with Flight Service. But most pilots want to know that there is someone whose job it is to monitor inbound VFR lists will be watching out for them.

There are circumstances where a flight plan of some kind is mandatory – be it IFR or VFR. These include flying across the Air Defense Identification Zone (ADIZ) from another country and flying in the vicinity of a VIP Temporary Flight Restriction. Both also require transponder identification codes and being in contact with Air Traffic Control.

You can file flight plans through a private vendor such as DUATs or with a Flight Service Station. DUATs allows you to go online and input the data yourself, but there are often glitches with the data getting through to the Radio you will activate with. The most common problem deals with time. Flight plans filed through DUATs do not transmit to Flight Service until an hour before the estimated time of Departure. If whoever inputs the flight plan miscalculates ZULU time, the flight plan will not be there. Many pilots get upset when that happens believing that the information should be available.

When DUATs does transmit a flight plan, only part of the data is sent. The rest of the data is not available to Flight Service unless the aircraft goes overdue – then the FSS sends a message to DUATs requesting the rest of the flight plan. Some Flight Service specialists will ask the pilots for their names and phone numbers when they activate the flight plan so that the information will be more readily available should the aircraft go overdue.

VFR Flight plans filed with any Flight Service in the continental U.S. are immediately available to whatever radio you activate with. If you forget to activate right away and call half an hour out or later, be sure to let the specialist know your departure point. Flight plans stay in the computer for two hours past the proposal time. If they are not activated they automatically drop out and the data is stored in the history files.

Filing a VFR flight plan also allows a pilot to organize his thoughts concerning the upcoming flight. It forces him to scrutinize his route and research what meteorological forces are in place that could help or hinder the flight.

A little note here about your family and the SAR process. One of the first calls made after determining that your aircraft is not at the destination airport is to the phone number listed on the flight plan. If that phone number is your cell phone – that's great. If it is your house phone and your mate answers, we try to tactfully ask if they've heard from you. Please let them know that a call from us does not necessarily mean anything except you haven't cancelled the flight plan yet. We usually just ask them to have you call us when you get in.

For decades pilot have used VFR flight plans for peace of mind. The system is time tested and works. The specialists at flight service are the most visible portion of the search and rescue procedure, but they are the vanguard of a nationwide team of aviation professionals who can be mobilized quickly when called upon. Notice that much of the information required by a flight plan is what you are required to give in order to receive a pilot weather briefing. If you call for a briefing, giving the flight plan first can save you time later unless you have a feeling that something might cause you to reroute or delay your flight.

```
Domestic US Flight Plan Information
*Denotes required information

*IFR or VFR
*Aircraft ID
*Aircraft type and equipment
*Airspeed
*Departure point
*Estimated Time of Departure (in GMT)
*Altitude
*Route of Flight
*Destination
*Estimated Time Enroute
Remarks
*Fuel on board in hours and minutes
Alternate Airports
*Pilot Information—Name, Home base of aircraft, phone number
*Number of people aboard
*Aircraft Color
```

IFR Flight plans are held in the database of the computer of whichever entity you used to file them until 1 hour prior to the time of departure, and then they are transmitted to the ATC computer system. If you filed with Flight Service you should be able to call the 1-800-WXBRIEF line and they can make any adjustments you need up to an hour prior to your departure time, and if it is later, they can call ATC for you to make adjustments to your IFR flight plan or they can file a new one for you. Flight Service cannot make adjustments to flight plans filed through DUATS, BASOPS, or any other vendor. If you needed one of those modified, Flight Service would simply refile for you.

The Change to ICAO Flight Plans

The International Civil Aeronautical Organization (ICAO) was created to standardize rules for aviation around the world so that pilots flying into other countries would not be confused. In the United States, ICAO flight plans must be filed whenever an aircraft is going to fly from one country to another over a major body of water.

In North America you can file using a domestic flight plan if you are flying across the borders of Canada or Mexico but departing and landing a U.S. airport, though you must always add the appropriate remarks and notify customs in advance. You can do this simpler flight plan as long as you are staying over land. For instance, flying direct from Brownsville, Texas (BRO) to El Paso, TX (ELP) direct does not require an ICAO flight plan because the flight path is over land the entire way. However, if you fly from Houston (HOU) to Brownsville (BRO) you will cross over the Gulf of Mexico and require an ICAO flight plan.

As the U.S. Air Traffic Centers bring the ERAM computer systems online, ICAO flight plans will become the norm for domestic IFR flights as well as international ones, but for now the FAA is starting slowly by only requiring a small segment of the aviation community to use this format. As of June 29th, 2010 the only domestic flights that are required to file an ICAO flight plan are those in which a pilot chooses to get preferential routing and use an RNAV standard instrument departure (SID) or arrival (STAR).

You do not have to file a domestic ICAO if you are simply flying an RNAV approach, to receive the preferential routings you must be on a STAR. Some pilots are confused by this. To see the difference, look at the approach plates for Atlanta-Hartfield Airport. If you are assigned the RNAV(GPS) Y RWY 9R approach, you do not file an ICAO flight plan. You do file an ICAO flight plan for the CANUK SEVEN ARRIVAL (RNAV). That's the easy way to tell, if it has a name, and says it is RNAV, then you should file ICAO. At this time pilots are not strictly required to file ICAO in order to use the preferential RNAV SID and STAR routes, it is done at the pilot's request.

In 1983 I began working as a controller trainee at Albuquerque Center. The computer in use at the time was the IBM9020 – a monster that took up a whole room. A friend of mine, a true computer geek, (and proud of it!) came to visit and I gave him a tour. As we walked into the computer room he exclaimed in awe -"A 9020…in working condition!"

Since that time the equipment has undergone improvements, and 2009 saw the implementation of a new computer system in the nation's Air Route Traffic Control Centers. The **ERAM** or Enroute Automation Modernization system being developed by Lockheed Martin will replace the Enroute Host system currently in use. The ERAM has the capability to determine exactly how closely an aircraft is following its flight plan, and be able to lessen those distances currently deemed "safe", thus increasing the efficiency of the ATC system. But in order to do this, the computer must know what level of sophistication each aircraft is capable of.

Conventional domestic flight plans do not have the extra fields that communicate this data to the ERAM, hence the use of the ICAO flight plan. The equipment portion of the ICAO flight plan, plus the data entered in the "other information" field, tell the ERAM the technological abilities of both the aircraft and the pilot.

By starting slowly, with one small segment of the aviation population, the FAA accomplishes several goals. They can field test the ability of the computers to accept the flight plans, they can "train" the pilots and the ATC personnel to think in terms of ICAO flight plan needs and they can do this without overwhelming the system before it is ready.

The FAA has decreed that all flight plans both domestic and International will be filed using the ICAO flight plan form by October of 2016. Many pilots are daunted by this, but it is not as formidable as it looks.

ICAO Flight Plan fields

- Aircraft Identification (Tail Numbers)
- Flight Rules (IFR, VFR or combinations of the two)
- Flight Type (General Aviation, Military, Non-scheduled Air Transport, Scheduled Air Service Other)
- Number of Aircraft (if left blank assume 1)
- Type of Aircraft
- Wake Turbulence Category
- Equipment—(a much larger list of options than in the domestic flight plans)
- Surveillance (SSR) - meaning type of transponder aboard
- Departure airport (4 letter ICAO—does not recognize letter/number combinations)
- Proposed Departure Time
- Airspeed in knots or Mach numbers
- Altitude: All flight levels prefixed by F (F370) below 18,000 ft. prefix with A (A120)
- Route: must put DCT between fixes with no airways. Do not include departure or destination airports.
- Destination Airport (4 letter ICAO—does not recognize letter/number combinations)
- Estimated Time Enroute
- Alternate Aerodrome
- Other Information
- Supplemental Information: Fuel, People Aboard, Pilot Data, Aircraft color, types of Radios, Survival Equipment, Life Jackets, Number of Dinghies, Capacity of Dinghies, Dinghy Cover, Dinghy Colors
- Optional Fields: Supplemental Remarks, Pilot in Command, Additional Addresses.
- Point of ADIZ (Air Defense Identification Zone) penetration. (L/L, FRD, or Location ID)
- Estimated time of ADIZ penetration.

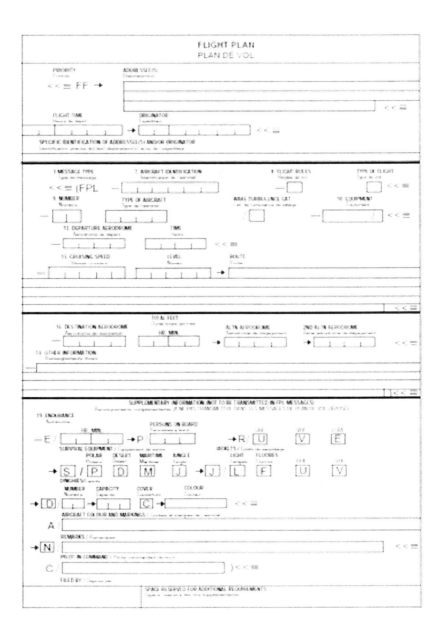

Extended Flights
The Pros and Cons of
Filing Multiple VFR Legs

Pilots planning to fly for an extended period of time frequently need to choose whether to file several flight plans or one long one. Which is better? The answer depends on the situation and, to some extent the reason flight plans are filed to begin with.

VFR flight plans are optional, with a few exceptions, such as when you fly across the Air Defense Identification Zone (ADIZ) on the U.S. border or through a VIP Temporary Flight Restriction. The VFR flight plan was created to help pilots in an emergency because it gives Flight Service and the Rescue Coordination Center (RCC) the information needed to find an aircraft if it does not arrive at its destination at the projected time.

Filing a VFR round robin or any extended flight plan, requires a decision as to how long you want to wait before help is sent if, for some reason, there is an emergency causing an unexpected landing. For extended flights of several hours, pilots will usually land for fuel, but often include the fuel stop in the estimated time en route.

If you file a flight for five hours—including the 30 minute fuel stop—search and rescue (SAR) will not begin until 30 minutes past your estimate time of arrival at the final destination. If the aircraft has a problem within the first hour of the flight causing an unexpected landing or an accident, a physical search will not begin for another four and a half hours. The role Flight Service plays in the early stage of SAR involves calling the destination airport, every airport for 50 miles either side of the flight planned route and all air traffic facilities to see if anyone has had contact with the missing aircraft..

Now assuming that you landed alive but injured in a snow covered wilderness only an hour after departure, the military and the civil air patrol will not launch search aircraft or vehicles for over six and a half hours. Statistics show that the sooner help arrives the greater the chance of survival, especially during weather extremes.

If you really do not like filing multiple legs, then be sure to contact some branch of air traffic along the route several times. If you can get flight following with Center during a portion of the flight then they will have a computer track that we can use in SAR. If you call radio for a weather update or a pilot report, there will be a record of your position. This narrows the search corridor considerably.

There is reluctance on the part of some pilots to file multiple legs, primarily because they are concerned that they will forget to activate or close each one. They are embarrassed if they go home to a panicked mate because flight service called to ask if they have heard from you, or if the FBO manager has to remind you to call. If this is the case, you may try a mnemonic device to trigger your memory. A popular option is to set a cell phone or other alarm device to the flight plan's ETA. When it goes off it will remind you to call Flight Service.

Also, this is the one area where Flight Service loves cell phone numbers. When you are filing your flight plan, list your cell phone along with your other contact information and that will be one of the first things we try to call to determine if you have arrived safely.

Most of the time flight service closes flight plans after calling the destination airport and discovering that the aircraft is on the field. Frequently the pilot never even realizes that he forgot to call us. This is easy when a tower or FBO is open, a little more difficult at a remote airport at night because the local police have to be dispatched to drive out and inspect the ramp. What is difficult for us is when an aircraft lands at a remote field when no one else is around and gets hangered – then we cannot find it as easily.

The preference, from the point of view of those who are responsible for Search and Rescue is for pilots to file multiple shorter flight plans rather than a one long one. Should an accident occur, this will not only begin the search faster but also limit the amount of terrain needing to be covered. SAR is generally for 50 miles either side of your filed route of flight.

The number one priority of flight service is safety and service to the pilot. Help us help you by filing multiple legs of your journey to ensure that SAR can more rapidly target your likely location in the event of an emergency.

The Black Hole
(Or where the heck is my Flight Plan?)

It happened again. While working Denver Radio a pilot called to activate his flight plan. I searched the proposal list, but there is nothing there with that call sign. The pilot was angry. "What do you mean it's not there? I filed it this morning with DUATS and this is the third time you guys have lost it."

Somehow pilots think when they file with the Direct Access User Terminal System (DUATS) or any of the other online services that take flight plans, they are filing with Flight Service and even if they've keyed something incorrectly, their company will still send the flight plan to Flight Service, or Center if it is IFR. This is not the case. DUAT is a separate computer system from both the Flight Service and Center/Tower systems.

There are actually a number of reasons why a remotely filed flight plan may be missing when you attempt to retrieve it. We will look over each of these and hopefully it will help to reduce the incidence of this happening.

The first thing to remember is that whenever you file a flight plan, it stays in the computer data banks of the company you filed it with until half an hour prior to flight time – then it transmits to the computer of the service provider, the Air Route Traffic Control Center (ARTCC) or Flight Service, with whom you will activate.

Say you filed IFR with DUATS. An hour prior to your proposed departure time the ARTCC or Tower will receive the flight plan – no earlier. If you call for clearance too early, or if your ZULU calculation was off, the flight plan will not be there. Flight Service receives VFR plans filed with DUATS an hour prior to the proposed time as well.

Flight Service does partner with some private venders such as ForeFlight, Aerovie and SkyVector – any flight plans filed with them do transfer to the Flight Service system. If the flight plan goes through vendors who partner with DUATs , Flight Service will never see your IFR flight plan. If you call an AFSS and ask them to change your proposed time or some other element, they do not have access to it. The best they can do is possibly call and see if the ARTCC has it already and pass along the changes or help you quickly refile.

Luckily Flight Service now has a website where pilots can file flight plans that do go directly into the Flight Service system free of charge. One of the primary advantages of a nationally linked computer is that if you have filed a flight plan with an AFSS, all the other AFSSs will be able to pull up the data. Flight Service can make direct changes to VFR flight plans filed with them right up until the time they are activated, and they can make changes to IFR flight plans up to an hour in advance of the proposed time – after that the flight plan transmits to Center so Flight Service no longer has control over it. www.afss.com is the website.

If you attempt to get an IFR clearance and the tower says the flight plan is not there, then call up the nearest Flight Service right away and see if perhaps it was accidentally filed as VFR. Changing it to IFR is a quick and easy fix, if that is not the problem, they will re-file for you.

Correctly converting to Zulu time is one of the biggest recurring problems. When I am speaking to pilots, I try to make sure that the time they give me is correct. Frequently a pilot gives me local time thinking I should automatically know what he means. Normally I will come back with something like "You mean tomorrow morning?" or "That's two hours from now right?" just to make sure that we are on the same wavelength.

Another major problem we have when it comes to IFR flight plans has to do with the way routes are filed. With the advent of GPS, a lot of pilots want to fly direct from departure to destination – and as long as those two points are within 300 miles of each other it mostly works. The Flight Service computers "know" where any fix in the country is, but the ARTCC computers do not.

ARTCC computers operate independently of each other – only meshing at the boundaries to the next ARTCC over. They know all the fixes and small airports in their own airspace plus about 200 miles outside their airspace. They also know all the major airports across the country.

ARTCC computers do not know where all the small airports or intersections or other fixes may be outside their designated airspace. Thus, if you have filed a flight plan with DUATS or Flight Service and it is a direct flight – the DUATS and FS21 computers will accept the flight plan, hold it until it is time to transmit to ARTCC, then transmit. At that point the ARTCC computer may reject the flight plan because the routing is not recognized.

This puts the flight plan into limbo. If it was filed with flight service and is kicked back to the AFSS, the flight data specialist may try to call the pilot with the phone number on the flight plan, or he may try to fix it and put FRC (Full Route Clearance) in remarks so than the person giving the clearance understands they are not to simply say "as filed". If it was filed with DUATs you may never know what happened to it.

One method of circumventing this problem is to simply file from your departure point to the latitude/longitude of your destination and from there to the destination. The Center computer always takes lat/longs.

Once you have "fooled" the computer and are airborne, you can ask the Center controller for direct to your destination and he can manually override it as he changes your clearance. Keep in mind that filing direct is simple, but if there are preferred routings in the ARTCC computer, it will alter your flight plan for you.

Flight plans seem like simple things, but computers are basically stupid – you have to spell everything out for them in a way they will understand. Hopefully this insight will help you in your next flight plan debacle or better yet avoid it from happening.

Creating a Pilot Profile

Living in the age of information means that whenever you log onto certain websites, the computer recognizes you immediately. This is a convenience to us as we do not have to continuously re-enter information. Developing tools intended to attract a technologically savvy customer base, Flight Service created a method for the pilots to obtain their requested weather briefings with less repetitive information provided to the specialist. It gives the briefers pre-stored information to provide a faster response to the pilot's needs.

The Pilot Profile is a data storage system designed to keep information on file in the flight service computers. Every time you file a flight plan there is data that is fixed and repetitive. This usually includes the aircraft call sign, type, and equipment, fuel on board, pilot name, phone number and home base.

Having this information pre-stored saves time during filing. The pilot profile also stores more complete data on emergency contacts. More than one aircraft can be stored, and a pilot who flies the same route over and over can save those flight plans for easy retrieval by the specialist.

Calling flight service from a stored phone number automatically inserts the pre-stored data into a flight plan mask. The data that is variable with each flight – departure airport, time, route, destination, ETE, Fuel, and number of people aboard, still need to be given to the specialist.

You can file a pilot profile by calling the pilot briefing line 1-800-WXBRIEF. The best time to file one is in the evenings – after 5 p.m local time. when general call volume is lighter and you are less likely to compete with fellow pilots preparing to fly. Advise the specialist you would like to file a pilot profile. They will ask you a series of questions covering all the data you choose to add.

One question you may be asked is your certificate number. This was designed to be an easy way to bring up your information originally, but that plan was abandoned when it was discovered that the older certificate numbers were also U.S. Social Security numbers. This box can be left blank since the specialist can search for a profile by using either the pilots name or any phone number used on the profile, or you can create one – such as a user name.

If your last name is common, specialists may end up scrolling through a long list. I suggest that you choose a "certificate" number easy for you to remember. If you are the sole owner of an aircraft, use that tail number. (Do not use it if multiple pilots use the same aircraft or if you own multiple aircraft.) Another option is to use your last name and a number, such as an area code. An example would be Smith505.

Whatever phone numbers you provide for the pilot profile will stimulate your information to drop into a flight plan mask. Your cell phone, home or office phone can be used, but only if you are the only pilot calling from those numbers. Whenever someone uses a "common source" phone number, such as an FBO number, data overload was occurring because that number could be used by numerous pilots. For that reason, FBO numbers are not accepted.

Flight Service has managed to speed up its ability to answer calls considerably since 2007 when the new computers went online. At that time the system was incredibly slow and many pilots became frustrated enough with their experiences that they sought other alternatives. The system has improved dramatically and currently the hold times pilots experience are normally under two minutes. Pilot Profiles help to speed the process as well, so give Flight Service a call at 1-800-WXBRIEF.

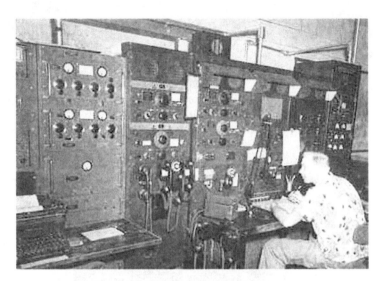

FSS RADIO 1951

Specialist Charles Andries working the

ABQ AFSS Radio position circa 2007

Chapter 16

The Evolution of
Flight Service Radio Communications

Before there were towers or centers, flight service was created to give pilots the information and peace of mind needed to perform a safe and efficient flight. Since its inception in 1920, what pilots know as Flight Service has undergone a great deal of change. Radio communication was a new thing back then, and the pilots calling simply stated the station name and "radio" to initiate contact.

At first, all the radio stations shared the same frequency, 122.2 VHF. Shortly the government saw that the field of aviation was growing so fast that it would be necessary to standardize the rules of the air across the nation. For a short time, it was under the control of the Bureau of Lighthouses, under the Department of Commerce, but by 1927 the Airways Division had been created. It was separated from the DOC in 1938 following the formation of a new government agency, the Civil Aeronautics Authority which eventually became the Federal Aviation Administration we know and love today.

In the meantime hundreds of small airports came into being as the wonder of flight spread into the general population. When an airport started having a steady stream of traffic, there became a need for a "Radio" station to give inbound pilots weather and surface conditions, and later to advise them of other traffic in the area. Radio gave weather to all overflights as well as handling information for the airport where the station physically existed, so separate discrete frequencies were assigned for pilots landing and taking off from that airport. This service was known as the Airport Advisory and included information about landing conditions on the field and other air traffic on the field or in the area.

Eventually towers were placed on really busy fields, but the smaller two- or three-man "radio" stations still gave Airport Advisories to the majority of airports across the nation. As the smaller Flight Service Stations were consolidated into the larger HUB facilities, Airport Advisory frequencies were remoted to the new locations and the RAA or Remote Airport Advisory took the place of the old AA.

As the science of radio allowed stronger transmissions, a problem developed. 122.2 VHF was initially the only frequency used at all the stations, and other stations were being set up very close to each other. The pilots could not always tell which station they were talking to, and if two different ground stations were keyed at the same time, the heterodyne effect blasted their ears. A range of discrete frequencies was assigned by the FAA for Flight Service use and the government began adding information concerning what frequencies were now assigned to what airport to their published airway charts.

Flight Watch was a separate service created in 1972 for one purpose only – to update weather for pilots en route between points on their current flight and to take pilot reports which are then transmitted to the National Weather Service offices. As for Radio, as mentioned earlier at one time there were Radio stations at any airport of consequence nationwide – up to 400 at one point. When advances in communication made it possible in the late 1980's, the FAA consolidated them into approximately one per state. At that point each Radio remotely monitored the frequencies left behind when they'd closed the stations at the various airports. I think it was a mistake to allow each of the Radio's to retain the name of the town it was physically located in at the time – it would have been less confusing to everyone if they could call out for "Oklahoma Radio" anywhere in the state rather than having to remember the name of the town McAlester. It would also reduce the confusion now that there is no longer a McAlester Radio in existence physically. Yet if you are flying in Oklahoma, "McAlester Radio" is what you still call to get service.

Both the Airport Advisory and Flight Watch services were eliminated in 2015 as technology offered other alternatives to the general aviation pilot. Radio is still available and the frequencies are listed on the FAA's low altitude IFR and sectional charts.

Their duties are as follows:

- Open 24 hours
- Handles FP processes (Activate, Cancel, Amend & File)
- Uses RCO's (discrete frequencies) and VOR Voices
- Relays IFR Clearances from Approach and ARTCC
- Helps lost pilots determine their positions.
- Required to always ensure pilots have adverse conditions enroute
- Assists pilots with inflight emergencies.
- Updates weather
- Issue beacon codes for customs
- Relay other information requested by pilots

Flight Service "Radio"

"Albuquerque Radio, N123, Over."
"N123, Albuquerque Radio."
"N123 request activate VFR flight plan."
"N123 roger, flight plan activated, Grants altimeter 30.01"

The Radio position in every flight service contains anywhere from 50 to 90 frequencies that the specialist on duty is monitoring. This is possible because most of the transmissions received are as short as the one above.

For example, at McAlester Service, the Radio (or inflight) position monitors VHF and UHF communication frequencies throughout Oklahoma. It also monitors VOR voices and both the VHF and UHF emergency frequencies.

Monitoring radios is not always a predictable or consistent occupation. During certain times of the day flight service can expect to receive higher numbers of calls then at other time, but there are long periods of time with no calls. Most of the time the specialist can keep up with any requests that come over these simply because the vast majority of contacts are of a relatively short duration – anywhere from 15 seconds to activate or cancel a flight plant to 3 or 4 minutes relaying an IFR clearance or coordinating a customs notification.

There are times when all these frequencies are active, especially during bad weather. Say an aircraft calls on the El Paso RCO and wants to update information for customs while crossing the border. A few seconds later you call on the ABQ RCO wanting to activate a flight plan. The specialist does not answer right away, so you call again.

The specialist may not hear you simply because in order to handle the call at El Paso, he has to mute the other frequencies (except the emergency frequencies which are never muted). If he tries to listen to all the frequencies at once, cacophony occurs.

The FAA requires that all aircraft be answered within 15 seconds, but as in the case shown above where multiple aircraft all call at once, this is sometimes impossible.

If communication never does get established, try calling another air traffic facility to see if perhaps it is the radio in your aircraft. If your radio is working fine on the other frequency, then be sure to contact Flight Service somehow to let them know one of their RCO's may be having problems

Another problem frequently occurs when a pilot tries to call using the VOR voice. Modern RCO's have made communication so easy that many pilots forget they need to listen to the VOR while transmitting on a different frequency, usually 122.1. It is very frustrating to hear a pilot who is obviously getting annoyed because he thinks he is being ignored when he is either trying to receive on 122.1, or has his VOR volume turned down.

There are a couple of other things that you as a pilot can do to keep frequency congestion to a minimum. Please do not file a flight plan on the frequencies unless you are airborne VFR and suddenly realize that to complete your flight you need to go IFR right now. Filing a flight plan for an upcoming flight is considered to be a preflight function and is lowest priority on the radios. There may be as many as four other aircraft standing by while a pilot who was not really prepared fumbled his way through a flight plan because he didn't feel like using a telephone or website.

Be prepared with any information you want to give or get before you make your call-up. Know where you are. Speak slowly and distinctly. If you are a student, practice speaking forcefully at home so that it doesn't feel odd in the airplane – try using a tape recorder and listening to yourself as you practice some of the routine calls you would make to Radio.

What kinds of things does Radio do? You already know that they help with Flight Planning - activate, amend, cancel, etc. They can update your weather and take PIREPS.

VFR Inflight Emergencies

One of the primary functions deals with inflight emergency services. Should a pilot become lost or disoriented, Radio specialists are trained in a number of ways to assist and are required to refresh that training quarterly.

You would think that the first thing to do would be to find the aircraft on RADAR—and you'd be right. Radio will first ask the pilot to squawk 7700—and then will call the ARTCC in that area to see if they can spot the signal flashing on their RADAR scope. If it is then the Radio specialist will relay the aircraft's position to the pilot and ask what his intentions, or requests, are now. Some pilots say "Thanks" and that's it.

However, it's not always that easy. A large part of the country does not have RADAR coverage below 10,000 feet and in some places even higher. Once it is established that an aircraft is not being seen by another ATC facility, the Radio specialist guides the pilot through various steps which will determine his location.

First Radio will ask some basic questions such as "What is your type of aircraft, altitude and are you in VFR flying conditions?" Radio can tell a general area where the aircraft is by the location of the receiver being used. Then Radio will ask if the aircraft has a working VOR or ADF receiver. Both of these can be used to cross fix the aircraft's position.

If the aircraft has no navigational equipment, Radio resorts to pilotage. While looking at a VFR sectional chart, the Radio specialist will ask the pilot for any significant landmarks. Helpful sightings include highways, power plants, windfarms, mountains, towns and waterways. Sometimes bad things can help as well—if he's flying in the west during the summer and sees a big forest fire , that is helpful.

Always let Radio know if you are low on fuel—they'll make it a point to search for nearby airports for you. Radio can also make phone calls for you in emergency situations and will help in any other way the pilot needs.

When a Radio specialist is involved with an emergency, he hands off all other radio traffic to another specialist and focuses on the pilot's needs. Keeping his voice calm and assured, he is able to project confidence to someone who is frightened and off balance. He will stay with them until the situation is resolved.

Relaying IFR Clearances

Another Radio function is to relay IFR clearances in areas where other ATC facilities have no radio coverage. The aircraft calls "Denver Radio, N3RK at Cortez requesting Clearance". Radio will verify the departure and destination points, then ask what runway the pilot wants and how long until he can depart. These questions are very necessary. Mistakes in airport identification can also be made when pilots and flight service people do not communicate all the necessary data. This can have serious consequences to safety when an IFR clearance is involved.

Though the pilot and the flight service specialist are both supposed to ensure the identification of the departure and destination stations, frequently a pilot will call for clearance off of an airport, but not give the alphanumeric designation of that airport or the state. They may simply say "Off of Peru going to Columbus".

A specialist working the Great Lakes area clearance delivery line will verify that the pilot means Bloomington, Indiana, not Bloomington, Illinois by naming the three letter identifier as well as the state. This works most of the time, but only if the pilot knows the identifier.

Once a pilot requested a clearance off of Greenville, South Carolina. He specified the state, but did not give the three letter identifier. When the FSS specialist called ATC for a clearance there was no flight plan. The specialist relayed that information to the pilot, who was annoyed, and a new flight plan was put into the system quickly. Based on the pilot's request, the identifier for Greenville, South Carolina was entered into the flight plan. ATC gave the specialist a clearance.

The Air Traffic center over Greenville, NORTH Carolina was not happy when this aircraft popped up into their airspace.

Who was at fault? The pilot who clearly stated South Carolina? Possibly. How about the Flight Service specialist who did not announce the three letter ID of the airport? That may have triggered the pilot to realize something was wrong. The fact that the flight plan was not available to the ATC facility in control of that airspace should have given both of them pause.

Another reason to always use the alphanumeric lies in similar sounding airport names combined with crackly radios or cell phones. There are six Pittstown, Pennsylvania airports and three Pottstown, New Jerseys. Not to mention a Potsdam, New York not that far away. Some of these airports use the same frequency to request clearance from flight service – so it is not a given that the specialist working radio will automatically know which airport you must be departing if you just say Pittstown.

Another reason for stating the airport or town name in addition to the three letter identification is because the letter combinations are frequently similar within a given state. For instance, there are four airports in Alabama whose identifications are a combination of either Zero, eight and Alpha, or O (oh) , eight and alpha. (i.e.: A08, 08A) Zeros and O's are often confused. It is wise to positively identify the destination airport as well so that when the specialist talks to the ATC facility controlling the airspace the correct flight plan is used. There have been instances where more than one flight plan was filed for an aircraft off of the same departure airport, but going to different destinations. Sometimes this is because two different pilots filed, or one flight plan was filed by a student and another by his instructor. Sometimes a pilot files using DUATS and an hour later decides to refile to a different destination without removing the first flight plan.

To ensure your safety, always state the alphanumeric identifier of the airports you are departing from and flying to as well as the airport or town name and the state. Positive communication only takes a moment, but it keeps us all out of trouble.

Declaring an Emergency

I have worked with a lot of pilots over the years. Students pilots, GA pilots, military pilots, air carrier pilots, all of them are, and should be, very proud of their flying abilities. Although I do silently chuckle when a pilot files his time enroute as "One hour and 29 minutes" I realize that being precise is necessary in aviation. There was one pilot – a Learjet – who actually filed 34 and a half minutes to Chihuahua Mexico one time, he was disappointed that the computer would not take fractions of a minute.

Unfortunately this also means that some pilots do not want to ask for help until the last minute. Declaring an emergency is an easy call if there is some catastrophic malfunction in the aircraft. It's those situations that are not immediately threatening or are somewhat embarrassing that I refer to.

Two of these pop to mind – getting lost and low on fuel. As I worked Flight Watch a couple months ago a VFR pilot called at 9:20 pm asking if I knew if he could get fuel at Goshen, Indiana at that hour. I had him standby and called the FBO – they were closed for the night. I asked if he was low on fuel and wanted to declare an emergency, but he said no, but asked me to check around other airports heading north from Goshen. He started sounding a little nervous, so after calling two others I called Kalamazoo approach.

They confirmed there was fuel available at that hour and gave me a squawk for the aircraft. The pilot dialed it in and Kalamazoo confirmed they had him on radar. He admitted he had minimum fuel, but at that point he was close enough to make it in.

Is this an emergency? The pilot did not say so, but once I heard nervousness in his voice I treated it as one as all air traffic control personnel are directed to do whenever the potential for an emergency exists. He had set out with headwinds and thought he had enough fuel to get to northern Michigan – a common experience.

When ATC feels a there is a possible emergency situation brewing, they take several actions. If possible, the first one is to offload all other traffic on frequency to another controller so they can concentrate on the needs of the aircraft in difficulty.

A lot of the emergency calls at Flight Service are from student pilots. Thank God for instructors who beat it into the trainee's brains that if they get lost just call 121.5 mhz. The first solo cross country flight is scary in a lot of ways and the worst that could happen to a student is if they are too embarrassed to call for help.

When I worked in El Paso there was an international flight school in Las Cruces, New Mexico. The instructors routinely made calling Flight Service to do a practice DF steer (remember those?) part of the curriculum. They memorized 121.5MHz as the emergency frequency. As a result when the students really got in trouble they knew who to call.

One day I got a call from a student – he was lost and below radar coverage. At that time I used his frequency and got a cross fix from the Guadalupe and El Paso DF's. It turned out he was 35 miles southeast of El Paso – in Mexican airspace. Once I told him that and got him turned north he also mentioned he was low on fuel.

While I spoke to the pilot, my co-workers called his flight school, US Customs and Border Patrol, and Air Defense radar to make sure everyone was aware that this was an emergency situation – even though the pilot did not declare it. This was not just a case of "minimum fuel" because of the potential for an international incident.

IFR or VFR, civilian or military, emergencies are taken seriously by all levels of ATC. Controllers are run through various scenarios during their training. Tower personnel have direct lines to their emergency equipment on the field. Flight Service specialists are taught several methods of locating lost aircraft using the navigation equipment on board your aircraft and keep VFR sectionals available to help with identifying local terrain.

All facets of Air Traffic must go through refresher training annually on how to handle hijackings, bomb threats, and several other potentially dangerous scenarios. They know that when an emergency is declared, the pilot will feel much more confident if the voice he is listening to maintains a calm and logical tone.

Who can declare an emergency? The Pilot, the aircraft owner, or an air traffic controller handling the aircraft. If possible, the first thing we do is ask the pilot to squawk 7700 on his transponder. If the aircraft is lost this is the fastest way to find him if he is within radar coverage. We determine the pilot's desires, then obtain enough information to handle the emergency intelligently. 121.5MHz is the primary frequency for emergencies, but we will work with an aircraft no matter what frequency he calls.

Whomever the pilot has contacted is supposed to keep him on their frequency unless a transfer to a different facility is in the best interests of the pilot. We try to keep communications open, but not overwhelming to someone who already is dealing with a stressful situation.

Once the situation is resolved, documentation is made by ATC and the specialist's handling of the incident is analyzed. If it was well done the specialist is recognized, if it could have been better he gets more training. It is gratifying when a pilot sends a compliment to the facility.

Whether your emergency is mechanical, weather related, being lost or some other factor, do not be shy about calling ATC. We take pride in helping you get home safely.

**The Direction Finder
used to locate aircraft in pre-radar days.**

Flight Service Specialists – ABQ AFSS Circa 1999

Chapter 17

Flight Service - Flight Data Functions

Mostly invisible to pilots, the specialists manning the Flight Data (FD) position in Flight Service provide the main point of contact for airport managers, Homeland Security, the Military, airshow managers, the Rescue Coordination Center and all other Air Traffic facilities. FD functions are varied and require a great deal of knowledge across many portions of the NAS.

FD initiates Search and Rescue on overdue aircraft, issues and cancels Notices to Airmen, relays information updates to Air Defense on aircraft entering the United States, and relays IFR clearances by phone for those airports without any radio communications outlets. Towers cannot enter PIREPs or weather observations into the NWS system, so when that information is received they call FD. If an ARTCC loses an aircraft on RADAR, they call the FD position to ask for assistance. FD has lists of every airport in the nation and the contact information for managers and local law enforcement. If a flight plan is misfiled by another specialist, the computer will kick it over to FD for correction.

Essentially Flight Data is the communications hub for the Flight Service program. When a pilot calls on the phone for an IFR clearance, FD takes the required information and calls the appropriate ARTCC or TRACON. They will then relay the clearance back to the pilot verbatim. Pilots departing from a non-towered field who flight service should give them the alpha-numeric designation of the departure and destinations airports as well as the name of the town and state they are departing from. There have been numerous instances of confusion over the airport identification that have resulted in operational errors and could have resulted in accidents.

When pilots call PIREPS into a tower, the towers have to call FD to input the data since towers do not have the capability. Many towers also call in the hourly weather observations. Flight data keeps track of aircraft that are inbound or proposed inbound to the United States— coordinating that data with Homeland security and customs.

There are several types of Notices to Airman, or NOTAMS. Distant (D) NOTAMS are issued by Flight Service. The National Flight Data Center puts out the FDC NOTAMS, and the ARTCC's issue NOTAMS for Temporary Flight Restrictions (TFR), including the ever popular Domestic Event Network TFR's (also known as VIP TFR's).

D NOTAM information is either called directly into the NOTAM position at Flight Service or sent electronically. The FD specialist takes the information sent by the issuer and formats it according to the National NOTAM handbook—FAA Order JO 7930.2M.

NOTAMs can be issued by Airport Managers, Airshow managers, parachute jumpers, communications tower operators, windfarm operators, RC aircraft enthusiasts, or anyone else having anything to do with an airport or with airspace. A stadium manager might issue a NOTAM if they are planning to launch a thousand balloons during the National Anthem.

Should you find yourself in a position to issue one, remember all the times must be in Zulu. NOTAMs concerning airshows, acrobatic practice areas, parachute jumping, unmanned aircraft, etc..may require a waiver from the Flight Standards District Office (FSDO). If you are planning any of these, contact them first.

Not just anyone can file a NOTAM for an airport. All airports must keep current lists of authorized issuers on file with Flight Service. The Flight Data specialists can receive NOTAM information via phone, fax or through the E-NOTAM system. All NOTAMs must be formatted according to ICAO standards so that all pilots flying in U.S. airspace can interpret them.

How VFR Search and Rescue Works

As a teenager, my father constantly reminded me to call him whenever I would be late getting home. If I was late he would start calling around to find me. Although this kind of monitoring by a parent is annoying, it is also a comfort to know that if something bad happened, he would be looking for me.

VFR pilots love to soar through unrestricted airspace, navigating their way without ATC telling them what to do. Yet the possibility of the unknown flies with them, and one way to mitigate disasters is to know that should the unexpected happen, Flight Service has a procedure to find lost aircraft and send help.

On a daily basis nationwide, Flight Service tracks between 20 and 40 pilots per day who simply forget to cancel their flight plans by the ETA. Of those, about half will call and close their flight plans within the first 30 minutes. That leaves about 10-20 who cause us to start looking for them. Also, if an aircraft is not on a flight plan, a relative, flight instructor or aircraft owner can call us to initiate the SAR process one hour after they had expected the aircraft to show up at his destination.

The first step taken in Search and Rescue (SAR) is to determine whether or not the aircraft has landed at his destination and simply forgotten

207

to cancel the flight plan. If they landed at a towered airport during the time the tower is open, it is usually a short search. If they land at an airport with an open FBO, the first thing we do is call the FBO, who very graciously sends someone outside to check all the tail numbers on the ramp. I cannot say enough about the patience and willingness to help we receive from the FBO managers everywhere.

Flight Service has lists of phone numbers for every airport in the nation. The airport manager's office is called next, but that is a business phone and if it is nighttime there may be no one there. The next call is to the local law enforcement. They will dispatch a unit to the airport to see if an aircraft matching the description and tail number given is on the ground. If it is, the flight plan is simply cancelled.

Many times pilots do not even remember the flight plan was not cancelled, and the aircraft was found, the lapse is not automatically forwarded to Flight Standards. The exception is a pilot who chronically forgets to close.

The first official step in SAR begins at 30 minutes after the ETA with a QALQ. This is a request sent by the destination AFSS to the filing facility, wherein we are asking them to send the whole flight plan. What most of you do not know is depending on who you filed with, we may not have your full flight plan when you activate. If you filed with any Flight Service we should have the data, but when you file with DUATs or another private vendor the only information we have is: VFR, Aircraft ID, type of aircraft, departure airport, destination airport, Proposed Time and Estimated Time Enroute.

When the facility which filed the flight plan receives the QALQ, they research their records for the flight plan and any subsequent contacts with that aircraft and squirt it back to a Lockheed Martin AFSS. The pilot data contains the phone number we will call. This is where we have come to love cell phones. We hate those things when we are briefing someone who is on a ramp in the wind with a noisy engine behind him, but they have significantly enhanced our ability to find someone who has simply forgotten to close a flight plan.

Frequently it is a home phone that is listed. If someone's wife or husband answers we try to identify ourselves and ask if they know where you are without alarming them. If no one is at the phone number, or if they do not know where you are, then we prepare to expand our search. Of course we leave a message with them to have you call us whenever you get in.

At one hour after the ETA the real work begins and we begin to be concerned that there is a possibility that you encountered conditions which forced you to land somewhere besides where you wanted to. An INREQ, or information request, is sent to all the Air Traffic Facilities along your route of flight, as well as the DUATS vendors, and we copy the information to the national Rescue Coordination Center (RCC) to give them a heads up.

All AFSS's, ARTCC's and DUATs are required to check their records to see if there has been any contact with your aircraft. It comes in handy if you have called Flight Watch and given a pilot report – which will automatically include a position report – or had any other contact with air traffic. If so, it narrows our search corridor from that point to your intended destination.

The pilot of a Piper Cherokee called Flight Watch to give a pilot report. He experienced engine failure and ended up injured in a tree. Compound fractures of both femurs broke the skin.   The Rescue team out of Jacksonville figured he would have bled to death in another 30 minutes. The pilot report took 200 miles off of the search area, which saved his life.

We are also required have ALL airports within 50 miles either side of your route checked to see if you have landed short. Do you know how many airports there are in southern California between San Diego and San

Francisco? If so, you have a clue as to how much effort goes into this step. This includes little dirt runways out in the middle of the desert as well as places as big as LAX.

Though this procedure normally takes more than an hour, if the pilot still has not been located and his ETA is exceeded by two hours, we must send out an ALNOT or Alert Notice. We continue with the communications search as the Rescue Coordination Center launches an air/ground search.

The Flight Service station that the pilot filed his flight plan with may at this point pull the tape recording of the briefing and flight plan and listen to it to determine if the pilot said anything that would indicate if he could perhaps have deviated from his route – or landed at another airport than the one on the flight plan. One pilot who had filed to a small airport late on a Sunday night, said on the tape that he was going to visit his Dad. He had filed to Clovis, New Mexico, but a check of the phone book found a man with the same unusual last name living in Portales, New Mexico – close by. Dad confirmed that Junior had come to visit. Turned out he hangered the aircraft because of storms in the area – which is why the sheriff could not find it.

An ALNOT remains current until the aircraft is located – or the Rescue Coordination Center gives up the search – usually at least three weeks. Again, if you are not on a flight plan, concerned family members can initiate the SAR process by phoning flight service. Be sure they have your Aircraft ID because all of our data is based on it – not on the pilot's name.

Statistics show that if people survive a crash landing, their chances are good if they can be located within 24 hours. I am asking you to help us help you by doing two things. File VFR flight plans that are less than 4 hours in length. The pilot who wants to save himself some effort by filing a 12 hour flight plan from Olivia, Minnesota to Medford, Oregon is doing himself a real disservice if he doesn't show up – that's one heck of a search area.

Please give position reports, better yet – give pilot reports. That way we will have a better idea about where to search. Please do not file the phone number of your FBO if you are landing at an airport 1200 miles away, cell phones or the name of the hotel you plan to stay with would be more practical.

---

*NOTE: If you crash land and your cell phone works – call 911 first!
Calling that number allows the local authorities to lock onto your signal and get a GPS reading of your location. Make that your first call – you can call Flight Service later.

SE-SAR - Surveillance-
Enhanced Search and
Rescue

SE-SAR improves the Search and Rescue
environment by adding surveillance data and
monitoring for indicators of an accident.

SE-SAR

Surveillance Enhanced Search and Rescue

Riding the breeze in your own small aircraft provides a sense of freedom and a lifting of spirit like nothing else. Yet, there is always the possibility that something can go wrong and you can't exactly pull over on a cloud when you hear your engine cough.

As mentioned earlier, Search and Rescue has been the primary responsibility of Flight Service for VFR aircraft since it was created in 1920. That is the reason behind filing a VFR flight plan, so if something forces you to land and you can't get to a phone, you always know that within a half hour of your ETA, flight service will begin looking for you.

That has been the way it was done for almost a hundred years, and it has saved many lives. The only catch is that they will not begin the search until after you should have reached your destination. If you have a four hour flight and are forced to land during the first hour, that means no one is going to start looking for three and a half hours.

Some pilots ask the Air Route Traffic Control Centers to follow them as they fly, and if the Center is not busy they will comply. It is not

213

mandatory for them to do so if you are VFR, and since VFR aircraft tend to fly low, they may terminate flight following because they cannot see you on radar. If you are on radar and suddenly disappear they must initiate search and rescue immediately if they cannot contact you. Over the past several years this has caused them to launch unnecessarily when a small aircraft simply went out of radar and radio range due to a low altitude.

Advances in technology now offer a better solution. There are several companies which have designed and are now selling satellite position reporting devices, like the one produced by SpiderTracks, which will send out a signal every six minutes as you fly along. The signal is picked up by satellite and relayed to a ground location.

Flight Service now offers a way for you to marry that technology with your flight plan to achieve the quickest and most efficient search and rescue process known for VFR aircraft. You can now file your flight plan (free) on the LMFS PilotWeb Portal (https://lmfsweb.afss.com/Website) and register your satellite position reporting device with Lockheed Martin Flight Service.

Known as Surveillance Enhanced Search and Rescue (SE-SAR), once you activate the flight plan, the flight service computer monitors your progress until you cancel the flight plan. At any point, if your signal stops moving, stops reporting, or you send an SOS, the computer alerts flight service and the Search and Rescue process begins at that point instead of hours later after your ETA.

The computer keeps a history of the signal as it tracks across the sky, which narrows the search area dramatically if a physical search is required. Because it is satellite based, not ground radar based, you can be flying at any altitude or over any kind of terrain. An icon of your aircraft shows up on their computer screen superimposed over the terrain with dots trailing behind it like bread crumbs showing the path you've flown.

One of the other advantages of using the PilotWeb portal for self-briefing and flight plan filing, is that you have direct control in activating and cancelling your flight plans. As you set up your personal profile you can register your email and click on a box that says EasyActivate/EasyClose. After that, whenever you file a flight plan you will get an email a half hour prior to departure with a link you can click and automatically activate the flight plan. Half an hour before your ETA another email is sent. Whenever you land you simply click that link to close your flight plan. You can still call on the radio or phone as well.

The PilotWeb is very easy to use, has great weather graphics and allows you to self-brief with all the same data that flight service has available. It also has the Airport Facility Directory and VFR/IFR chart information loaded and easily available. There is a plan language option called NextGen which will spell out the meaning of TAF's and FA's if you don't want to work at interpreting the National Weather Service's abbreviations.

Surveillance Enhanced Search and Rescue is the next logical step in making it easier for people to find you if things go wrong. It's a safety net that provides peace of mind to you and to your family, knowing that you can fly cross country anywhere and those whose purpose is to be there for you in an emergency will be able to find you with greater ease and efficiency than anytime before.

Indianapolis Tower circa 1964

Air Traffic Control Towers
History and Overview

If you ask the general population where Air Traffic Controllers work, they will point to the tall, elegantly tapered structure rising high above an airport. It is their only real reference to ATC outside of movies and television. The people in the ATC Towers are responsible for aircraft and other vehicles on the ground or in the air around a specific airport.

Back in time we travel to the 1920's. After WWI Americans went crazy over the concept of traveling through the sky. Weekend mechanics began constructing aircraft in their barns, the government put together cross country routes for air mail, and businesses discovered how convenient it was for both people and products to travel quickly between places.

Aircraft could just land on any straight, flat piece of earth, but municipalities quickly discovered that to attract lucrative businesses, they should develop dedicated landing fields. This created new sources of employment: people to maintain the runways and airfield, aircraft mechanics, structures where pilots and passengers could sit, make calls, and get a snack. Large airfields with such amenities, coupled with primary locations around large metropolitan areas, ensured increasing numbers of transient and locally based aircraft. By the end of the 1920's there were 145 municipally owned landing fields in the United States. With no such thing as onboard radios the pilots had to depend on their own powers of observation to make sure they had the airspace and runways to themselves.

Unfortunately this frequently resulted in near misses or actual aircraft accidents over areas with dense traffic. In 1929, an aircraft mechanic named Archie League made up two oversized flags — one green and one black/white checkered. He took them out on the St. Louis airfield and local pilots were taught that green meant "go ahead", the other one meant either "go around" if they were flying, or "Hold in Place" if they were on a taxiway getting ready to take the runway. Archie is acknowledged as the first official Air Traffic Controller.

1929 Archie League, the first air traffic controller, on duty at the St. Louis airport

By this time most of the aircraft used for personnel or parcel transport were being equipped with radios and in 1930, Cleveland Municipal Airport began using them to control the traffic on the field. Light guns were developed for those planes not equipped with radios. These had red and green filters to signal a pilot whether or not to proceed. Airlines had most of their aircraft equipped with radio by 1932.

Towers were independently operated. All hiring and training was done locally and procedures varied from airport to airport. In November of 1935 the Department of Air Commerce hosted a conference including representatives from all segment of the aviation community to discuss the possibility of a uniform air traffic control system. But it was not until March of 1936 that the director of Air Commerce, Eugene L Vidal, was able to convince Congress of the necessity for the Federal Government to take over Air Traffic Control.

An Air Traffic Control Section was created under the Department of Air Commerce in January 1938. Its job was to standardize Air Traffic Control Tower Equipment, and Operation techniques, and issue certifications for both the facilities and the personnel.

In 1938, the Civil Aeronautics Act created an agency independent of the Commerce Bureau, the Civil Aeronautics Authority (CAA). In 1941 the CAA was authorized federal funding to construct and operate ATC towers, and soon the CAA began taking over operations at the first of these towers, with their number growing to 115 by 1944. Also in 1944 Ruth V. Osgood, a pilot, became the nation's first woman air traffic controller when she was hired at Chicago's Midway Tower.

Then there was RADAR! In 1952 Radio Detection and Ranging equipment used radio waves to detect distant objects. Installed in darkened rooms inside the Control Tower facilities, RADAR allowed controllers to regulate air traffic around busy airports. The first RADAR pictures were fuzzy green blips on a black background. They were laid flat like tables. Controllers standing over the top of them had clear plexiglass markers called "Shrimpboats" laid on top of the RADAR returns. They used black grease pencils to mark the aircraft callsign and altitude on the shrimpboats. The RADAR antennas were positioned close to the center of the airfields and the screens had range rings drawn from the center so that controllers could tell how far out the aircraft were. This portion of a tower was called the Approach Control.

Early RADAR picked up rain and snow as well as aircraft, so any weather system moving through the area greatly diminished the ability of controllers to tell where the aircraft were. Nonetheless, when a target was identified as inbound, the RADAR controllers used shout tubes to call up to the Tower Cab and tell them from what direction an aircraft was arriving.

Tubes were used to send messages from the tower down to approach. 1 inch by 8 inch strips of paper were attached to plastic sleeves and dropped down the tube. These messages contained the information on aircraft which the tower had just given clearance to depart the field.

1960 saw the installation of the ASR-4 Airport Surveillance radar at Newark. This system had a range of 60 miles, and was capable of seeing up to 25,000 feet. Newark was also equipped with ASDE-2 radar, which allowed controllers to view the ground positions of aircraft and vehicles on the airfield regardless of the weather.

Nov 5, 1962. FAA announced a standardized design concept for Air Traffic Control towers, featuring a free standing tower with greater visibility from the cab, improved spaces for radio and radar equipment and a better environment for ATC personnel. This was created by NYC architectural firm I.M. Pei and Associates.

1965 the ARTS (advanced radar traffic control system) computer programs were field tested at Atlanta Tower. The most exciting part of the ARTS system was that it electronically tagged radar targets with the Aircraft ID and Altitude – Goodbye Shrimpboats!

In 1970 the FAA established the Terminal Control Area concept. The TCA was designed to minimize the midair collision hazard around the nation's busiest airports. Pilots flying in these areas were required to have onboard radios and be in contact with ATC at all times. And in 1976, the FAA introduced the Air Traffic Control Handbook, the 7110.65. This was a compendium of all procedures, phraseology, and regulations used by controllers nationwide.

As technology advanced so did the number of aircraft wanting to land and depart at any one time. The pay scale for Tower Controllers was directly tied to the number of "operations" on the airport daily. Controllers would normally begin their careers at the smaller airfields and bid into positions larger facilities as slots became available.

After the airlines began using the HUB concept—wherein they tried to get all their aircraft to arrive and depart any given airport at the same time, the government began instituting "flow control" restrictions on airlines in 1985.

Terminal Approach Control facilities (TRACONs) were increasingly split off from single airports. With the ability to remote the radar information, one TRACON can handle several airports. SoCal TRACON handles over 45 airports in southern California.

In 2004, the FAA awarded contracts for the management of Level 1 and 2 towers to SERCO. Other companies competed for these contracts over time. All privately managed towers must comply with the same rules as those run by the Federal Government.

In the U.S. today there are 264 air traffic control towers; 162 Terminal Radar Approach Control Facilities TRACONs and six Operations Support Facilities. Air traffic controllers are generally well organized, have assertive and firm decision making skills, and possess excellent short-term memory and visual memory abilities. In addition, studies have shown that controllers generally have a degree of situation awareness that is much higher than the average population.

These skills give pilots confidence that they will be safely guided through the crowded skies.

A Note on Tower payscales.

The federal pay grades for Tower and TRACON controllers is directly linked to the traffic Level of the facility. In most cases the FAA hires controllers to work lower level towers. If a person wants a higher paygrade, he has to bid when an opening becomes available at a higher level facility.

Higher level facilities mean higher levels of stress as well—so at some point you have to ask yourself how much money do you really want?

Tower and TRACON Operations

All Air Traffic Control Towers, large and small, serve two primary directives—keep aircraft and other vehicles on the surface and aloft over a specific airport separated and maintain an efficient flow of air traffic.

In smaller towers there may only be two people on duty during the busiest times of day. Whereas, by contrast, moderate to larger towers will have every position staffed but may have only a few on duty during the hours of midnight to 4am.

There are 12 levels of Air Traffic Control Towers, which are determined by the average number of operations run in a 24 hour period. The largest include Atlanta, Georgia, Los Angeles, Chicago's O'Hare and of course, New York LaGuardia. The smallest towers may only have one controller on duty at a time and close at night—these include places like Hobbs, New Mexico.

The positions listed below are basic to all towers, and usually coincide with the various frequencies a pilot uses. In the case of smaller facilities, or during periods of low traffic, one person may handle more than one position. The basic position list includes:

- Flight Data
- Clearance Delivery
- Ground Control
- Local Control
- Tower Coordinator
- Supervisor

Only airports with higher density traffic will also be covered by a Terminal Radar Approach Control or TRACON. A TRACON's airspace may only cover one airport, or it may be primarily be dedicated to one airport but the airspace will cover other smaller airports. The largest Approach Controls cover airspace over several large airports. For instance, Southern California (SoCal) Approach starts north of Los Angeles and covers the western third of the state all the way south to the Mexican border. These TRACONs may not be in any way connected to a specific tower or even located on airport grounds as all their communications, data lines and

RADAR imagery are relayed remotely.

TRACONs frequently separate their airspace into Departure Control and Approach Control. As soon as the aircraft wheels have lifted from the ground, the pilot switches frequency to speak to the Departure Controller. (DC). The DC follows the aircraft as it ascends layer by layer until it either reaches the edge of the TRACONs airspace laterally or vertically. Departure routings are distinct from Arrival routings, which allows for safer pathways.

Aircraft entering the TRACONs airspace speak to the Approach Controller who vectors the aircraft into lines three miles in trail aimed at specific runways. They will issue speed restrictions and if an aircraft is too fast or slow, they may turn the aircraft out of the line up and give him a new position in line.

Overflight aircraft are also under direct control as they must be vectored to avoid the traffic entering and exiting the airports covered by the TRACON.

All the controllers in a facility are expected to "check out" on—or become operationally proficient in every position in the facility. New hires or controllers who have transferred in from other facilities are rotated through all these positions until they become certified as a Full Performance Level (FPL) Air Traffic Control Specialist.

In the next few pages we will look at the operational positions in a tower and TRACON. We begin with the first frequency a pilot will listen to when he wishes to depart a towered airport—the ATIS.

Tower Operations Flight Data Functions

The specialist manning this position receives the computer printout of expected flights—both incoming and departures—and passes it on to whichever position the aircraft will speak to first. If it is a departure it goes to the specialist at Clearance Delivery. If it is an inbound, it will initially go to a sector in the TRACON, if there is one, or to the Tower Coordinator.

Flight Data records and monitors the information being broadcast over the ATIS—(Automated Terminal Information Service), this is a continuous broadcast of non-control information such as weather and NOTAMs at the airport. In some Towers, Flight Data takes weather observations which are then called into Flight Service for dissemination.

Normally pilots do not speak to the flight data specialist, though in some airports, this function is combined with the Clearance Delivery position.

All pilots departing or landing at the airport are required to monitor the ATIS in order to obtain the most current information. The ATIS must be updated at least once per hour and more often when weather or NOTAM information is updated. Each broadcast is designated with a phonetic letter from the aviation alphabet—and ends with the instruction for the pilot to advise the tower he has received the information.

For example: *"Advise you have information Romeo"*

Flight Data will pass along relevant information to the other positions in the tower concerning any ATC delays, clearance windows or anything they receive involving the National Airspace System as a whole. They coordinate NOTAM information with airport management and/or flight service. If a tower receives a pilot report, the FD specialist will call it into Flight Service.

At the end of the day, FD collects any paperwork related to the day's traffic and files it away for management to look over in the morning.

Tower Operations Clearance Delivery

Before an IFR aircraft even leaves the gate the pilot usually calls

Clearance Delivery to receive confirmation that his flight plan is in the system and has been approved. The Clearance specialist will specify which departure procedure the pilot should take to fit smoothly into the traffic patterns aloft, give the initial altitude the pilot may ascend to, and ensure the pilot has the appropriate frequencies.

"A-T-C clears Aerostar three romeo kilo from the Albuquerque airport to the Wichita Falls Airport via the Albuquerque three departure Tucumcari transition, then as filed. Climb and maintain one-seven thousand, squawk 2734, contact Albuquerque approach 126.3 upon departure."

If the flight is to an airport subject to flow control restrictions, the Clearance will inform the pilot of the window of time in which he is required to depart, or let them know when a ground delay is necessary.

Pilots sometimes file flight plans with routes that are not allowed because they conflict with established routings. An example would be a route that exits controlled airspace in the face of inbound traffic patterns. When that flight plan is forwarded to the Tower from the Centers main computer it will have an alternate routing spelled out in big red letters. Instead of saying "As Filed" - the Clearance Delivery specialist will read the entire alternate routing to the pilot. Pilots are expected to read back the clearance instructions to ensure accuracy.

If a pilot has a special request for his departure, Clearance calls the appropriate control facility with an Approval Request or APREQ. For instance, during a slow period one time we received a request from an F15 for an afterburner climb up to thirty three thousand. Clearance told the pilot the climb was "on request". The F15 pilot must take the standard clearance limits given unless he receives further instructions from the Local controller

Clearance relays the request to the Local Controller and the Tower Coordinator. The Coordinator then APREQs the request with the TRACON and/or the Center whose airspace lays above the TRACON.

Sometimes clearances will be to points short of the aircraft's destination. In the section on Air Route Traffic Control Centers (ARTCC or Center), we will look at the alternate clearance limits.

VFR aircraft must also call Clearance to get a transponder code prior to departure. They are required to let Clearance know in which direction they will depart. Clearance passes that information to Ground Control. As long as a VFR aircraft is on the grounds of a towered airport, or within the TRACON's airspace, it must obey the tower's instructions.

Tower Operations Ground Control

The Ground controller monitors all aircraft and other vehicles transiting the airport surfaces. In larger airports there may be more than one Ground controller, or if it is a Hub airport for a major airline, the airline itself may control the surface traffic within an area where only the Companies aircraft and equipment operate. That is why you will occasionally see two towers at a large airport.

Ground control gives taxi instructions to aircraft from the terminal to the runway and vice versa. They also give airport management vehicles permission to cross runways. Smaller airports require the Ground controllers have visual contact with the airport surface at all times. Some larger airports have a radar that sees vehicles on the ground. Ground control must notify Local control when a departing aircraft has been taxied to a runway other than one previously designated as active.

Ground ensures that aircraft and other vehicles do not taxi on or across runways—unless the Local Controller has approved. Information concerning the movement of surface vehicles must be transmitted to the pilots transiting the area.

When aircraft have taxied to the departure end of the runway the Ground controller gives Local the flight information strips lined up by the order in which the aircraft are waiting to be released.

HUB Airport Variations

Large airports frequently serve as HUB facilities for major air carriers. In some cases the company will rent a very large section of the terminal and have their own ground control facility to monitor and control surface aircraft and other vehicles—such as baggage trains. The company may get clearance information and transmit it to their pilots. As the aircraft is taxiing to the edge of the company's area, their ground controller will turn over control to the ground controller at the tower.

Local Control or "TOWER"

Pilots call this position "Tower". Local Control gives instructions (Clearances) allowing aircraft to taxi onto the runway and depart or land. His is the final authority over the runways and the airspace immediately over the airport. The Ground controller will request approval from Local prior to issuing instructions to any aircraft or surface vehicle to cross a runway.

Larger facilities will have a radar monitor bright enough for the Local controller to see the direction of arriving aircraft. In smaller ones, the controller depends on really good eyesight.

Tower Coordinator

The Coordinator backs the Local Controller up by performing the interfacility coordination via interphone and ensuring the control instructions are recorded. They will communicate control requests and instructions to the TRACON or the overlying ARTCC (Center). The Coordinator position is used primarily during periods of increased activity and assists the Local controller in performing his primary function.

Supervisor

In the Tower cab, the Supervisor provides an extra pair of eyes to monitor all positions. Supervisors maintain currency on all positions and can take over any position in the cab at need. He makes sure that the controllers have breaks and when things get busy he will activate the Coordinator position. He ensures that operations run smoothly. The Supervisor also ensures that the controllers receive their refresher training and are briefed on new information, bulletins, and changes to rules and regulations related to their job.

Air Carriers are supposed to taxi slowly for safety reasons. One late afternoon there was a Southwest Airlines jet being followed down a taxiway to the terminal by a Delta flight. Southwest was dawdling because another aircraft was still parked at his gate.

Though the pilots are NOT supposed to make unauthorized transmissions, the following exchange was heard.

"KNOCK, KNOCK—GET THAT MUSTARD COLORED AIRPLACE OUT OF MY WAY!"

A few moments later the Southwest replied. "We are NOT mustard colored, we are yellow and orange and WE carry Texas GOLD all the way to the bank!"

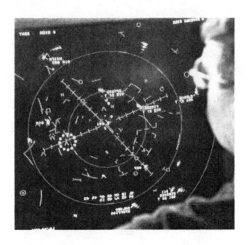

Terminal Radar Approach Control

TRACON

A Terminal Radar Approach Control or TRACON is only located at airports with high traffic densities. They control aircraft in the airspace above an airport that has a significant amount of local traffic—both landing/departing and overflights. Their RADAR is usually located on the field—which allows the most precise returns. This gives them the ability to run aircraft closer together than the Centers—three miles apart at the same altitude instead of five.

Aircraft wishing to enter the airspace owned by a TRACON must contact them prior to entering to give their intentions and receive a discrete transponder code which identifies the aircraft on radar. Upon entering a TRACON's airspace, a VFR aircraft must obey instructions given by the controller just as an IFR aircraft does. If landing, they will be put in sequence with IFR traffic.

When departing the TRACON will track VFR aircraft until they have left their airspace, then let them change frequency and squawk VFR (1200). IFR aircraft are kept until the Centers assume control at the TRACON's boundaries.

Most TRACONs are physically located in the base of a Tower, but today's technology allows TRACONs to be in a completely separate location. This is the case in places where there are many busy airports in a small geographical area—such as Southern California.

Where a TRACON is co-located with a Tower, the Controllers usually work both facilities—Tower one day and TRACON the next.

During busy periods the TRACON's airspace can be divided into several geographical and/or altitudinal areas with controllers watching different RADAR screens. Major airports will have one or more controllers assigned to inbound traffic only, and another assigned to departures.

TRACON airspace size varies according to the needs of the area. A small TRACON, such as the one in Roswell, New Mexico may be part time, with the overlying Air Route Traffic Control Center taking over its responsibilities at night.

At a minimum there are three positions active in a smaller TRACON during the day, but there could be several of each depending on the size of the airspace. The Radar Positions, The Data (D) side positions and the Assistant or A-side position. Of course, a supervisor is also normally on duty on the operations floor.

TRACONs are large dark rooms with several RADAR screens. Lights are kept low. Each RADAR position has a computer keyboard and tracking mouse. Next to it is the DATA position, with its own keyboard and a rack containing strips of paper—one for each aircraft currently in, or about to enter the airspace. These strips show pertinent information on each flight such as routing, altitude and type of aircraft. The

232

Assistant is normally a mobile position, collecting the data as it comes off the printer, and disseminating it to the correct location.

Let's look at each position closely.

TRACON — Radar Positions

During the night all RADAR positions may be run from one location, but for the most part a TRACON's airspace is divided into sectors regulating traffic into and out of the airspace.

Each TRACON is different - different boundaries, different altitudes, different preferred routes in and out of the airspace. The Radar are set up to focus primarily on one area. Although the rules overall are the same – as dictated by FAA Order JO7110.65 – how they are applied must be flexible.

The TRACONs serving larger airports have it easier in some ways than some of the mid level traffic facilities. For the largest airports, like Atlanta International, all the inbound flights are set up to come into the airport at least 5 miles in trail over specific fixes beginning hundreds of miles away. Also many of the largest airports do not allow small aircraft or helicopters to land. Even so the sheer volume of traffic is challenging.

The TRACON's radar controllers have to set up the inbound flow for the Tower controllers. The most difficult traffic patterns involve ones where all the different kinds of aircraft come into the area from all directions. Large air carriers, fast fighter jets, small experimentals, businessmen in Bonanzas, politicians in Learjet's, military cargo planes plus helicopters can play havoc with setting up a line of aircraft all wanting to land in a half hours' time!

Additionally they keep aircraft simply transiting their airspace away from the ones descending or climbing. They thread the departing aircraft upwards to the edges of the TRACON airspace and turn them over to the Center, or if VFR – turn them loose.

TRACON – D-Side Controllers

Like Centers, the TRACONs have two controllers at each position during busy times. While the RADAR controllers eyes are glued to the scope, the D-side is coordinating actions with the surrounding sectors. Anytime an aircraft needs to do something that will affect the next controller's airspace, the D-Side calls them over what is called Service B – direct lines – to APREQ an action. An Approval Request (APREQ) may be for a WAFDOF (wrong altitude for the direction of flight) or a deviation to the planned route because of thunderstorms.

He or She will also be a second set of eyes for the Radar controller and insures that aircraft coming into his sector are flying the routes and altitudes expected by scanning flight strips. The strips may also tell
him things that he needs to alert the Radar controller to – such as if an aircraft is wanting to do practice approaches, or cannot conform to speed restrictions.

Symbols	Meaning
T→ ( )	Depart (direction, if specified)
↑	Climb and maintain
↓	Descend and maintain
→	Cruise
@	At
X	Cross
‑M→	Maintain
⇗	Join or intercept airway/jet route/track or course
=	While in controlled airspace
△	While in control area
⤳△	Enter control area
⊘△	Out of control area
NW⊘ ⊘ NE ⊖→ E	Cleared to enter, depart or through surface area. Indicated direction of flight by arrow and appropriate compass letter. Maintain Special VFR conditions (altitude if appropriate) while in surface area.
250 K	Aircraft requested to adjust speed to 250 knots.
-20 K	Aircraft requested to reduce speed 20 knots.
+30 K	Aircraft requested to increase speed 30 knots.
Ⓦ	Local Special VFR operations in the vicinity of (name) airport are authorized until(time). Maintain special VFR conditions (altitude if appropriate).
>	Before
<	After or Past
170 (red)	Inappropriate altitude/flight level for direction of flight. (Underline assigned altitude/flight level in red).
/	Until
( )	Alternate instructions
Restriction	Restriction
↓	At or Below
↑	At or Above
-(Dash)	From-to (route, time, etc.)
(Alt)B(Alt)	Indicates a block altitude assignment. Altitudes are inclusive, and the first altitude shall be lower than the second. Example: 310B370
v <	Clearance void if aircraft not off ground by (time)

NOTE: The absence of an airway route number between two fixes in the route of flight indicates "direct"; no symbol or abbreviation is required.

Since most aircraft travel between four and eight miles a minute, there is very little time to write out variables and information that needs to be passed on to other sectors. Symbols that are fast and easy to recognize and decipher are penciled onto the flight strips.

If there is more than one airport in the TRACONs jurisdiction, the D-side controller may get a call from Flight Service requesting a clearance from a small field that has no frequency directly to the TRACON. The D-Side controller consults the RADAR controller and they determine what heading and altitude the departing aircraft will need to be doing – then he gives Flight Service the clearance instructions to pass on to the pilot.

Clearance instructions are written on the flight strips using the standard symbols – they become a way to remember what was given, a quick reference for other controllers and a record of activity.

TRACON – Assistants

An assistant controller in the TRACON environment mostly lends a hand with keeping the flight strips organized. Their duties are varied and supportive – taking calls from Flight Service personnel who are looking for overdue VFR aircraft or creating the ATIS recordings which pilot monitor prior to landing.

Tower Support Staff

The management team of any air traffic facility is responsible for ensuring that the ATC operational personnel have everything they need to perform well—from training to adequate breaks. The functions in a smaller tower may all be combined—with the manager also performing supervisory duties. In general, all towers must have one or more people responsible for:

- Managing the facility and people over all.
- Supervising operations
- Training—both initial and ongoing
- Quality Assurance

Chapter 19

Talking to Air Traffic Control

Student pilots have a lot to absorb about aviation. Ground school, aircraft instruments and capabilities, weather and once all that is all of a sudden you have to pick up a microphone and talk to Air Traffic!

Figuring out what to say and how to say it without sounding stupid is a challenge- the Tower and/or Flight Service can usually tell a new student within three words. To prepare yourself (or your students) there are several steps you can take.

First, be very familiar with the aviation alphabet. (alpha, bravo, charlie, etc...) Standard phraseology was developed because radio transmissions are not always clear. The other aircraft and the ATC controllers are listening for certain things, if you speak in a non-standard way, ATC may not understand what you want.

Get used to hearing yourself talk. Practice with a tape recorder going over some of the more commonly used phrases. Speak distinctly and slowly. One of the most common student errors is to rush the contact, which muddles communication. Do not be afraid to ask the Tower or Flight Service specialist to slow down – let them know you are a student and they will go out of their way to work with you.

As you practice speaking into the microphone, envision the flight. Mentally do your preflight check list, get in the plane and strapped in. Have on a clipboard next to you all the frequencies that you will probably be required to dial into the radio. Including UNICOM, Flight Service, ATIS, Approach, Tower and Ground Control. Crank up the engine. Visualize picking up the microphone and dialing the local UNICOM frequency into the radio. Listen first for a moment in case someone else is calling in .Now speak into the microphone as you depress the button, "UNICOM, Skyhawk one-two-three four Foxtrot (remember to say the numbers individually) taxing from Cutter to Runway 8." Don't forget to let go of the button.

Taxi to the runway, keeping a look out of the windows to see any other ground traffic. Once you have reached the runway and looked to see if anyone is landing or departing, you pick up the microphone again and announce your intentions.

If you have a flight plan, you will want to dial the flight service frequency into the radio. "Bridgeport Radio, this is Skyhawk 1-2-3-4foxtrot, departing Sterling, over." Remember to give your position on initial call up. Sometimes more than one frequency will light up on Radio's console and you want them to use the one closest to you for clarity.

If Radio or any other ATC facility does not answer immediately, it may mean that they are talking to another aircraft on a different frequency, or that they are coordinating something on the landlines with another ATC facility. Wait about 30 seconds and try again. If you have tried three times and not received an answer, check to make sure your volume is up and the correct frequency dialed in. If it is, and you have a backup radio, try using that one. Eliminate the possibility of mechanical problems on your end first. If another frequency for radio is in the area, try using that one – just in case the

Remote Communications Outlet (RCO) is down. If you still cannot get radio, then try contacting the Center. They can relay your request to Radio and inform them that the RCO does not seem to be working.

AFSS: "Skyhawk one-two-three-four foxtrot, Bridgeport Radio."

PILOT: "Radio, Skyhawk one-two-three-four foxtrot departed Sterling, request activate flight plan to Bradley"

AFSS "Skyhawk 34 foxtrot, roger flight plan activation, verify you have the AIRMET for turbulence enroute."

PILOT: "November 34 foxtrot has AIRMET for turbulence."

AFSS: "November 34 foxtrot roger, Bridgeport altimeter two-niner-niner-eight.

All transmissions from you and from the ATC facility you are speaking to must be prefaced by your call sign. This eliminates the possibility that other aircraft in the area may think ATC is talking to them. Notice that after the first transmission, you can drop the first two numbers in the call sign. You can also use November rather than your aircraft type. But whichever way you do it be consistent.

Before you call Bradley Approach dial in the BDL ATIS frequency to listen to the weather and NOTAM information on the field. Make a note of the ATIS letter designation. Just before Approach's boundary, dial in the approach frequency, pick up the microphone and depress the button.

PILOT: "Bradley Approach, November 1-2-3-4 foxtrot, thirty-five northeast with Information Romeo."

APCH: "November 1-2-3-4 foxtrot, Bradley Approach."

PILOT "November 1-2-3-4 foxtrot, inbound VFR for landing at Bradley International."

APCH: "November 3-4 foxtrot, roger, squawk one-three-four-five, turn right heading one-two-zero vectors to runway three. , Bradley altimeter three-zero-zero-four"

PILOT "November 3-4 foxtrot, squawking one-three-four-five, turning 120 degrees, three zero zero four."

Think of all the options that Approach could give you and practice responding aloud while visualizing the physical actions you need to take to comply. Keep an ear out for Approach to call you and give you the next instruction. You already know that he will be giving you a frequency for Tower shortly, so be ready to dial it into the transmitter.

APCH: "November three-four foxtrot, contact Bradley Tower one-two-four-point-seven."

PILOT: "November three-four foxtrot, roger."

Dial in the new frequency, wait to see if anyone else is talking, then:

PILOT: "Bradley Tower, Skyhawk one-two-three-four foxtrot turning final for runway three, over."

TOWER: "Skyhawk three-four foxtrot, roger, cleared to land runway three, Bradley altimeter three-zero-zero-four."

Once you are cleared to land Tower will not normally address you again until you have touched down because they know that landing and departing takes all your concentration. Once you are on the ground they will tell you to contact ground control and give you a frequency. Change to that frequency for taxi instructions.

The language seems stilted and formal at first, but when you find yourself dealing with a lot of ATC instructions and radios alive with static, communication will be greatly enhanced when you know what to listen for. ATC greatly appreciates pilots who correctly and clearly use the language of aviation.

Frequency Congestion

Have you ever called for Radio, Tower or Center and had no answer? You are pretty sure your radio is working and the volume has been turned up, so you call again and there is still no answer?

If you are on the right frequency for the area, there may actually be a number of reasons why this can happen. Some are the result of equipment limitations, and some are related to radio procedures.

We will start with Radio. The Radio position in every Flight Service contains anywhere from 50 to 90 frequencies that the specialist on duty is monitoring. For example, at the DCA Flight Service Hub, the person working the DCA inflight postion (radio) monitors VHF and UHF communication frequencies throughout Virginia, North Carolina, West Virginia, Pennsylvania and parts of New York. It also monitors several VOR voices and both VHF and UHF emergency frequencies.

During certain times of the day Flight Service can expect to receive higher numbers of calls then at other time, but there are long periods of time with no calls for long periods of time. Most of the time the specialist can keep up with all requests simply because the vast majority of contacts are of a relatively short duration – anywhere from 15 seconds to activate or cancel a flight plan to 3 or 4 minutes relaying an IFR clearance or coordinating a customs notification.

There are times when all frequencies are active, especially during bad weather. Say an aircraft calls for entry into the Washington SFRA. A few seconds later another aircraft calls at RDU wanting to activate a flight plan, but the specialist does not immediately answer. He may not hear the second aircraft simply because in order to handle the call for the SFRA he has to momentarily mute the other frequencies (except the emergency frequencies which are never muted). If he tries to listen to all the frequencies at once, cacophony occurs.

The nice thing about the new FS21 computers that Lockheed designed is that the frequencies are now all linked into a computer screen. The main page of the screen stays blank until someone calls over a frequency – then that frequency appears on the screen and stays there until the specialist activates it.

The FAA requires that all aircraft be answered within 15 seconds, but as in the case shown above where multiple aircraft all call at once, this is sometimes impossible.

If communication never does get established, the pilot should try calling another air traffic facility, such as Flight Watch to see if perhaps it is the radio in his aircraft. If your radio is working fine on the other frequency, then be sure to contact FSS somehow to let them know that one of their RCO's may be having problems.

Another problem occurs when a pilot calls over the VOR voice. Modern RCO's have made communication so easy that many pilots forget they need to listen to the VOR while transmitting on a different frequency, usually 122.1. It is frustrating to hear a pilot who is obviously getting annoyed because he thinks FSS is simply not answering him, when he is either trying to receive on 122.1, or has his VOR volume turned down.

Pilots are required to always give their position on initial call-up. We understand you may not know which facility to call for, so go ahead and just call for Flight Watch, as long as you tell us where you are reference an airport or NAVAID. Please do not say you are over Hobokan lake – I may not know where that is, but I pretty well better know where the VORTACs are in my airspace.

There are a couple of other things that you as a pilot can do to keep frequency congestion to a minimum. Please do not file a flight plan on the frequencies unless you are airborne VFR and suddenly realize that to complete your flight you need to go IFR right now. Filing a flight plan for your next flight is considered to be a preflight function and is lowest priority on the radios. We have had as many as 4 other aircraft standing by while a pilot who was not really prepared fumbled his way through a flight plan because he didn't feel like using a telephone!

"Hey there...it's my turn!"

In aviation, as in life, we sometimes wonder how we rate. How does Air Traffic Control determine who gets priority handling?

When I began my training at Albuquerque Center in 1983, FAA 7110.65 – the "Bible" of Air Traffic, stated it simply. Service is on a first come, first serve basis except that priority shall be given to

· Aircraft in Distress

· Lifeguard Flights

· Presidential Aircraft

Over the years the Federal Aviation Administration has added several categories of aircraft that should get priority handling. Looking at the roster I am reminded of the procession list of a royal parade.

First come, first serve is still at the top of the list, with aircraft in distress and Lifeguard flights as priorities one and two. Number three, aircraft involved in a search and rescue mission, was slipped in before Presidential aircraft.

After that we have a raft of minor functionaries jostling for attention. FLIGHT CHECK, is followed by NIGHT WATCH, then FLYNET, GARDEN PLOT and SAMP aircraft. All of these are government aircraft;

FAA, NOAA, or military. After them, ATC is supposed to expedite the movement of interceptor aircraft on active air defense missions. To be honest if I was any of the others so far, I'd probably stand back and let him go first. I prefer staying behind the guy with the guns.

Once he's gone, the next priority goes to the aircraft called SCOOT, then TEAL and NOAA. IFR aircraft have priority over SVFR aircraft and finally the OPEN SKIES observation and demonstration flights are given priority over all "regular" air traffic.

A comforting note at the end of the section indicates that priority is given to any aircraft that has been diverted for any reason.

So, basically, once you've finally gotten to taxi to the runway that had been closed by an emergency landing, you will not be given a clearance until the Lifeguard departs and the President lands. Once airborne you will be vectored around FLIGHT CHECK and under NIGHT WATCH, , then FLYNET will cause you to circle around GARDEN PLOT, while SAMP, takes your requested altitude.

The wake turbulence behind an intercepting SCOOT aircraft will bounce you across the paths of TEAL and NOAA to OPEN SKIES where you will get priority handling as a reward for being diverted.

Now doesn't that make you feel warm and fuzzy all over.

There are other priorities that are not covered by this section, but which are simply practical. For instance, at an uncontrolled airport, IFR aircraft that are inbound have priority over aircraft sitting on the ground requesting IFR clearance to depart. If it is a VFR day, the aircraft on the ground could choose to depart using VFR rules and pick up his clearance from the ARTCC once airborne.

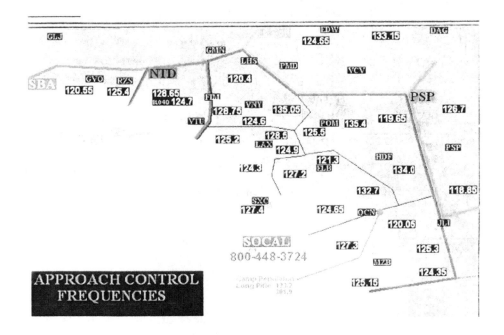

APPROACH CONTROL FREQUENCIES

Transferring Control

Airspace is divided into geographical areas and altitudes. Yes, there are uncontrolled areas still in existence, but for the most part each piece of airspace is controlled by a specific Air Traffic entity. At a small towered airport, the tower "owns" only the area close into the airport. Larger airports will have Approach/Departure controls and then of course we have the Air Route Traffic Control Centers.

Have you wondered how everyone keeps up with who is supposed to be watching your aircraft? A combination of communication, radar, and procedures are used to define responsibilities. In IFR conditions,

249

your flight plan is instrumental in allowing ATC to sequence their actions prior to your call for clearance.

Most Towers are linked by computer to the rest of the ATC system. If there is no associated Approach Control, the Tower will call the Center to get your clearance after you leave Tower's airspace. When you depart, they key this information into a computer, or they call the Center to notify them of your departure. The Center keeps the airspace around that airport clear until you are identified on radar and in communication with them.

If the tower has an Approach Control, specific departure procedures are set so that the Tower does not have to coordinate every flight. The Center's computer has assigned the squawk code which the aircraft is given while receiving clearance. The Tower gives clearance to depart and change frequency. As soon as the aircraft leaves the airport surface squawking that code, Approach picks it up and radar identification is made. At that moment, Approach assumes control of the aircraft. They will follow it to the outer limits of their airspace.

As the aircraft approaches the invisible boundary of Approach airspace, the equipment starts flashing the data block on the radar screen to alert the controller. Simultaneously the equipment at the Center receiving the equipment will pick up the signal and also flash to alert that controller of an incoming aircraft. If no further coordination is required, the Center controller keys the accept key and the Approach controller has the aircraft change frequencies.

If the Center controller sees a problem with the aircraft approaching his airspace he immediately calls the Approach controller to have the aircraft put on an alternate heading or altitude before it enters his airspace. Only after the Approach controller makes this change does the Center controller accept the handoff.

For instance, an air carrier departs Amarillo, Texas eastbound. The Fort Worth boundary is fairly close at hand so the air carrier is normally still climbing to his requested altitude. Fort Worth sees the aircraft handoff, but has traffic at FL260. Fort Worth calls Albuquerque Center and asks that the air carrier be stopped at FL250. If Albuquerque is talking to the aircraft they will comply and Fort Worth accepts the handoff. If the aircraft is actually still on frequency to Amarillo Approach, Albuquerque will call them to relay the information prior to accepting the handoff. Fort Worth will allow the air carrier to continue his climb once the conflicting aircraft is no longer a factor.

The further ahead an action to avoid aircraft coming into conflict can be taken, the easier it is on the pilots. For instance if the computer shows a potential conflict 200 miles from the conflict point, one or both aircraft may be asked to alter their heading by only 5 degrees, then be set on course once the required separation is achieved. A more drastic diversion ordered less than 20 miles apart would spill everyone's drinks and cause a lot of yelling.

The same procedure for coordination is used as the aircraft transits between Centers or between the various sectors within the Center's airspace. Each Center is huge – covering many states and altitudes, so the airspace is broken up in a manner that allows the greatest efficiency. For instance Albuquerque Center covers most of west Texas, New Mexico and Arizona. The airspace around Roswell is full of military operating areas, but the Restricted Airspace of White Sands Missile range does not allow east-west travel by aircraft at any altitude. Because of this there is little commercial air traffic in the area – mostly military and small aircraft. That chunk of airspace is usually kept whole from the surface to FL600 as the controller is primarily concerned with military maneuvering.

All major east-west flows must either transit over El Paso or about 60 miles south of Albuquerque. The corridor south of Albuquerque eastbound is the initial sequencing point for all the airports in the Dallas/Fort Worth area. The airspace there is stratified so that aircraft above FL240 going to those airports can be lined up and fed into a stream. Albuquerque Center has a letter of agreement with Fort Worth Center that aircraft heading into the DFW metroplex from the west/northwest will all transit over Texico VORTAC no less than five miles apart. The Fort Worth controller expects these aircraft and steers his other traffic away from this path. By the same token, aircraft heading west from El Paso are fed into streams for Phoenix, San Diego, or Los Angeles.

The radar screens of both the current and receiving facilities begin flashing the aircraft's icons at least 20 miles before the aircraft reaches the boundary. Under the Aircraft's ID there is an H plus the sector number or Approach control identification flashing. H23, means that the handoff is to Sector 23, HABQ is handing off to Albuquerque Approach. Some of the Approaches have amusing combinations – whenever a handoff is made to El Paso Approach the icon flashes "HELP".

Wake Turbulence

In the late 1960's the effects of what had been described as "prop wash" or "jet wash" was recognized as a serious flight hazard which was examined and identified officially as Wake Turbulence. A natural result of powered flight, the disturbance of air trailing behind aircraft greatly increased in strength as the greater size and speed of wide body turbojet aircraft were developed.

Vortices generated by wake turbulence are of such strength that an aircraft traveling behind the one creating the vortices can be forced into a roll from which it cannot correct or recover. Accidents and incidents attributed to wake turbulence are a significant contributor to worldwide safety statistics.

Wake turbulence includes vortices, thrust stream turbulence, jet blast, jet wash, propeller wash, and rotor wash both on the ground and in the air. In flight it is caused by a pair of counter-rotating vortices trailing from wing tips. They are circular patterns of air created by the movement of an airfoil while generating lift.

Vortex strength, or rotational force, is governed by aircraft weight, wing shape and speed. Larger aircraft produce greater force than smaller ones. The shape of the wing refers to the loading capacity of the wing, or how many pounds per square foot the wing is required to support.

It is interesting that at higher speeds the airflow over the wings is spread out and smoother. It is the slower speeds, with a greater angle of attack, that create a greater chance for the wake to form.

Vortices from large aircraft sink approximately 300 – 500 feet per minute. They level off at approximately 500 – 900 feet below the flight path, and slowly move outward because lift forms first at the root of the wing and then develops toward the wingtip. To avoid contact with this effect smaller aircraft should remain behind and above larger ones in flight.

In the course of any flight, the effect begins when an aircraft rotates while taking off, and ends as it lands. When possible, aircraft landing behind larger aircraft should stay at or above the larger aircraft's flightpath and note where it touches down. Land beyond that point, runway length permitting. If unable to do so, the smaller aircraft should delay landing for a couple minutes, perhaps by doing a go around.

Vortices slowly descent and diminish in strength with time and distance. When close to the ground with *no wind*, vortices will move laterally outward at 2 – 3 knots. A delay of at least two minutes after a heavy aircraft executes a low approach, missed approach or TGL will greatly decrease the effect.

Similarly, when departing, it is best to delay the departure for a couple minutes. You should also note the larger aircraft's rotation point and do not begin the take-off roll unless your rotation point will be **prior** to the larger aircraft's rotation point.

At airports with control towers, FAA Order 7110.65 mandates aircraft 12,500 lbs. or less must not be cleared for takeoff behind larger aircraft for at least three minutes after the larger aircraft departs.

Helicopters also produce wake turbulence as high pressure air on the lower surface of the rotor blades flows around the tips to the lower pressure region above the rotor blades. In a slow hover taxi or stationary hover near the surface, helicopter main rotor(s) generate downwash producing high velocity outwash vortices to a distance approximately three times the diameter of the rotor.

When rotor downwash contacts the surface, the resulting outwash vortices have behavioral characteristics similar to wingtip vortices of fixed-wing aircraft, but instead of being down and out, helicopter circulation is outward, upward, around and away from the main rotor(s) in all directions. This circulation when upwind of a runway can drift towards the runway. Pilots of small aircraft should avoid operating within three rotor diameters of any helicopter that is in a slow-hover taxi or stationary hover.

In forward flight, departing or landing helicopters produce a pair of strong, high-speed trailing vortices similar to wingtip turbulence of larger fixed-wing aircraft which can affect small aircraft while operating behind or crossing behind landing and departing helicopters.

Other factors that can affect the strength of wake turbulence include whether or not the larger aircraft is departing or landing on another runway – either crossing or closely parallel. A steeper than normal descent or an aircraft landing slower than normal will increase the effect as well. Wake turbulence decays faster if there is atmospheric instability, such as strong low level wind flow at the surface or turbulence aloft.

Wake turbulence is the invisible enemy – you have to realize that the potential for it to exist is there and make decisions based on observation and knowledge of its characteristics.

References: FAA Wake Turbulence Training Aid, April 1995, and Air Traffic Bulletin, Issue 00-6, Fall 2000.

Chapter 20

Air Route Traffic Control Centers

History and Overview

In each of 22 buildings across the U.S., in rooms big as a football field, as many as 100 air traffic controllers are actively watching the skies over their assigned territories at any given time of day or night. Unlike the towers and approach controls, the Air Route Traffic Control Centers (ARTCCs or "Centers") are not associated with any specific airport. They were designed from the very beginning to regulate air traffic over large areas from just above the surface to as high as their equipment can function (about 60,000FT) .

It began back in the 1930's. The steel magnates and auto industry had begun using air travel heavily from Chicago to the east coast. Construction

257

of airports with good runways and services also encouraged the development of airline travel. Though aviation was only a couple decades old, the skies were already becoming crowded. Radio communications had been set up with the Airway Radio Stations (ARS)-the precursor of today's Flight Service, and the airlines had set up other radio transmitters/receivers from the Great Lakes to Newark and Washington D.C.

Although the government was aware that something needed to be done, they did not have the money or congressional approval to do anything – so the airlines created a method to track their aircraft, built a central communications structure, and hired people to run it. In 1935 the first Airway Traffic Control Center opened in Newark, New Jersey. Within six months there were ATCC's open in Chicago and Cleveland.

The Air Commerce act of 1936 gave the government the powers to take over the administration of all three Centers, and to construct new ones as needed. If you look at a map of the Centers, the first thing you notice is their odd shapes – they definitely do NOT conform to state boundaries. The airspace was defined according to the areas most used by pilots at the time. Future facilities were defined the same way, so that the Center maps look like a big patchwork quilt.

There was no RADAR when this all began. In the Centers, geographical maps with the locations of navigational aids and airports (what we call Sectionals today) were laid on top of a large table, and overlaid with glass. Small markers called "shrimp boats" representing aircraft were pushed along the routes of flight which they had filed prior to flight. As aircraft passed over various checkpoints they called the Centers, or the ARS, or whatever Air Traffic Facility had receivers in the area and gave their positions. If the ARS or Airport towers took the position they would transmit the data back to the Centers via telegraph or telephone. The Center controllers would move the markers based on the filed route and airspeeds.

How can you actually control aircraft if you can't see them? What made it more challenging was that not all aircraft flying were participating – only the airlines. General Aviation was so prevalent it wasn't even a category at that time. Nonetheless, the controllers of the day developed methods to keep track of the aircraft and would relay instructions to keep them separated based on altitudes and speed/time/distance calculations. These non-radar techniques were still be taught as the first phase of air traffic control instruction when I went through the academy in 1983.

A big shakeup in governing aviation came under the Roosevelt administration. In 1938 the Civil Aeronautics Act created an agency independent of the Commerce Bureau – the Civil Aeronautics Authority. FDR also split the CAA into two agencies – one oversaw the actual control of air traffic, airports, aircraft certification and airway development, the other was entrusted with accident investigation, safety and the economic regulation of the airlines.

1941 saw the advent of a new method of air navigation, Very High Frequency omnidirectional radio range (VOR), initially installed at an experimental station in Indianapolis. Using the new system, a pilot could remain on course by watching a dial on his instrument panel, and he could give the ARTCC controllers valuable information – the exact radial he was reading on the VOR.

RADAR!!!   In 1952 Radio Detection and Ranging (RADAR) dramatically improved the ability of the controllers to determine aircraft position.   Early radar saw aircraft, but it also saw rain, making it difficult during storms to see aircraft…but it was a start.

By 1965, 42 million people, or 38% of the adult population of the U.S. had flown in a commercial aircraft. It was not until 1967 that technology advanced to the point where early computers were married to RADAR to electronically tag the aircraft with it's ID, altitude and airspeed. The IBM 9020 computer took up a large room, and was still in operation through the 1980's. In addition to the radar display, the computer took over the task of mathematically determining how long it would take an aircraft to transit its route, and would print out strips for the controllers with those calculations.

1976 saw the implementation of the Conflict Alert System into the ATC computers.   Known to controllers as the "snitch patch", this program provided a visual and audio alert when it sensed the potential for aircraft flight paths to intersect resulting in a loss of separation.

The aftermath of the union strike in 1983 meant a nationwide slowdown in aviation as the government dealt with the problem of how to handle aircraft with one third its original staff.   It also defined a need for better methods of achieving an efficient flow into the major airports – especially those that served as hubs for airlines. In 1985 the FAA published rules for Flow Control wherein aircraft were issued takeoff and landing reservation times at high traffic density airports. Center controllers were required to set aircraft up five miles in trail along specified pathways into high traffic airports beginning hundreds of miles away from the destination.

The next level of technology to dramatically affect aviation was the Global Positioning Satellite (GPS) method of determining position. Up to this time IFR aircraft were routed along pre-determined airways.   GPS allowed pilots to fly direct from beginning to end – which they loved, but controllers did not. Imagine all cars on the road, taking each turn in a calculated manner, but now one jumps the curb and drives across a field then wants to jump back onto the road between two Mac trucks! Aircraft can't just stop and wait for the trucks to pass...

So what's next? ERAM technology, being installed at the Centers now, is the heart of the Next Generation Air Transportation System (NextGen) helping to advance our transition from a ground-based system of air traffic control to a satellite-based system of air traffic management. The FAA is studying the feasibility of having GPS based computers on the ground giving direct control instructions to the computers in the aircraft. This would allow tighter spacing and greater efficiency of air traffic – and reduce the need for human intervention.

It's only been a hundred years since the sound of an aircraft engine added a new note to the symphony of the sky. Step by step we've created the most advanced aviation system in the world. I wonder what the next decade will see.

Microwave towers relay radio transmissions hundreds of miles from aircraft in flight to the ARTCC.

Air Traffic Control Centre in 1960's showing air traffic control enroute sector positions. Aircraft position reports received from pilots were regularly updated onto paper-stripboards.

ARTCC Operational Positions and Responsibilities

Each ARTCC is almost a small town in and of itself. Surrounding the control floor are administrative, training and technical staff offices. There are locker rooms, break rooms and an onsite cafeteria serving over 300 controllers and their support staff. In addition to between 40 and 60 radar positions, the operations floor contains space for managerial areas, Flow Control, military liaisons and National Weather Service specialists.

The geographical area covered by each ARTCC spans several states and is divided both geographically and by altitude. In areas of dense traffic one geographical area may have different sectors controlling aircraft below 18,000FT MSL, another controlling the altitudes between 18,000FT and 28,000FT and a third position controlling aircraft 29,000FT thru 60,000FT. 60,000FT is the top of the Positive Control Area and does not fall under the jurisdiction of ATC.

Flow Control monitors the activity in and around the entire ARTCC airspace, along with weather patterns. They also keep track of the flight planned proposal times of other aircraft wanting to join the dance aloft. If projected volume exceeds established parameters, or if weather causes difficulties in certain areas, the Flow controllers will initiate departure or arrival delays.

Each sector in the ARTCC airspace will be monitored by one to three people at a time during the course of the day. The practice of airlines to land their fleets together as close as possible to reduce the passengers ground times causes air traffic to increase and decrease in waves. At the busiest times each sector may have one person (R-Side) who monitors the RADAR and speaks on the radio to the aircraft, a second (D-Side) controller responsible for handling communications with surrounding sectors and other ATC entities as well as watching the lists of aircraft about to impact the sector, and a third controller assisting and overseeing all actions.

Also on duty are several Flight Data assistants who ensure the accuracy of information as it comes into the facility before being disseminated to each sector.

During times when traffic is very light—such as during midnight shifts—one person may handle all those duties for one or more sectors.

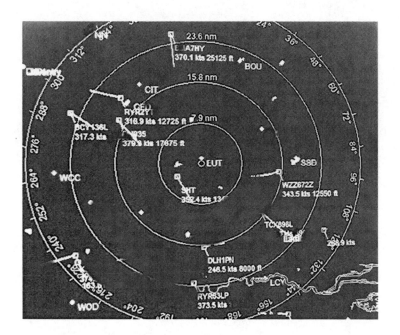

RADAR Position

Each RADAR screen in the facility can show just one sector or be expanded to include the surrounding sectors as well. This comes in handy for midnight shifts when sectors are combined or during emergencies such as when Chicago ARTCC was shut down after an intruder started a fire in the facility. In that case the sectors from Indianapolis, Minneapolis and Kansas City ARTCCs which abutted Chicago ARTCC expanded their RADARs to cover Chicago's airspace.

The Radar screens have toggle on/off switches to display the airways and fixes in the area as well as significant weather patterns. Air Traffic RADAR is normally set to minimize weather displays unless there are major systems transiting the area. Separate monitors in each grouping of sectors are set to display weather continuously.

Aircraft show up as small arrow like icons with data blocks appended. Controllers can extend a line forward along the route of the aircraft to see if it will conflict with other aircraft. The data blocks contain the Aircraft's Identification, Altitude, Speed, the aircraft's computer generated ID. The data block will flash whenever the aircraft approaches the boundary of the sector's airspace, simultaneously the flashing block will appear on the next sector's or TRACON's radar with the ID of the next sector flashing in place of the computer ID. For instance, when Albuquerque (ZAB) Sector 23 is handing off to Fort Worth (ZFW) sector 17, the ZAB sector will see H-A17 flashing and the ZFW will see H-F23 flashing until such time as ZFW "accepts" the handoff manually. If the next sector does not accept the handoff prior to the aircraft reaching the next boundary, the sector in which the aircraft is currently flying is required to keep the aircraft in their own airspace. Of course prior to that happening the Sector controller will call the next sector to find out why the handoff has not been accepted.

When handing off to an approach control, the data block will flash H (for handoff) plus the ID for that facility. When ZAB hands an aircraft off to ELP TRACON, the data block flashes H-ELP until the Approach controller accepts it.

The rules of the air for Centers are that aircraft must be separated by at least five miles laterally at the same altitude or by 1000 feet vertically. If aircraft at the same altitude look to be converging, the computer will generate a 5 mile ring around those affected alerting the controllers to a possible situation. In Air Traffic parlay, a "near miss" means the aircraft came within that five mile ring.

Each sector has a unique VHF and UHF radio frequency, as well as access to the emergency frequencies in their areas. They can toggle on the frequencies for surrounding sectors when combined. There are direct access communications with other ATC sectors and facilities as well as computer interfaces.

Contrary to what people may see in the movies, the national Air Traffic Computers are separated from all normal internet functions in order to eliminate the possibility of intrusion by hostile entities.

The RADAR Associate or "D-Side" Controllers

During most daylight hours there will always be a second person assigned to each sector whose function is primarily communications. While the Radar controller is talking to the aircraft, the D-Side controller is coordinating with all the surrounding sectors and facilities. For instance, and aircraft requests a descent to another altitude. If the aircraft is already close to the border of the sector's airspace the D-Side will call and APREQ (request approval) from the next sector prior to the Radar controller issuing the descent instruction to the aircraft.

The D-Side controller monitors the flight strip information on all the aircraft currently on the sector's RADAR as well as the strips for aircraft half an hour away. Early knowledge of how many aircraft and what pathways they are flying will give the sector controllers opportunity to mitigate problems before they arise. If the D-Side sees two aircraft at the same altitude but coming from different places have the potential for conflict as they enter the sector, he can reach out to one or both of the other sectors and request assistance in changing the aircraft's heading or altitude to ensure separation.

Before the advent of RADAR, rules for separation dependent on speed, heading and distance were created which are still taught at the academy before controllers are taught to use the RADAR. The flight strips monitored by the D-Side controllers show a fix within the sector's airspace and what time the aircraft is expected to transit that fix. If for some reason the RADAR were to go down, the D-Side controller who has been monitoring the flight strips takes over issuing control instructions to the aircraft using those rules.

During the course of the day a pilot experiencing weather anomalies might tell the RADAR controller what is happening. The D-Side may either enter the data into the weather service computer or pass the Pilot Report to Flight Service.

Radar Coordinator Position

As mentioned earlier, during times of heaviest traffic a third person will work with the RADAR and D-Side controllers. This person will assume the coordination responsibilities with other positions allowing the D-Side to concentrate on the information generated on the flight progress strips. The D-Side can also then provide a second set of eyes on the RADAR and point out potential problems to the RADAR controller.

Flight Data Assistant or A-Side

The Flight Data assistant ensures information coming into the ARTCC is complete and accurate before it is posted to the sectors. They coordinate non-control information with other air traffic facilities. For instance, Flight Service may issue a Notice to Airman about upcoming parachute jumping activity. They alert the ARTCC Flight Data position who then makes sure the appropriate sectors are aware of when and where this will take place. Flight Service may also call the ARTCC Flight Data position to modify proposed flight plans. Since Flight Service is the only publicly published phone number, pilots will call them and ask if the time on a previously filed IFR flight plan can be changed. Flight Service may have to call the ARTCC Flight Data specialist to update the information.

GENOTs/RENOTs or "General/Regional Notices" disseminated by the FAA regional or national operations centers come into the Flight Data computers along with Temporary Flight Restrictions and other information important to air traffic. The Flight Data assistants determine which sectors or staff members could be affected by the information and distribute it accordingly.

ERAM Implementation
and
ICAO Flight Plans

In 1983 I began working as an ATC control trainee at Albuquerque Center. The computer in use at the time was the IBM9020 – a monster that took up a whole room. A friend of mine, a true computer geek, (and proud of it!) came to visit and I gave him a tour. As we walked into the computer room he exclaimed in awe —"A 9020...in working condition!"

Since that time, the equipment has undergone improvements, and in 2009 began the implementation of a new computer system in the nation's Air Route Traffic Control Centers (ARTCCs). The ERAM, or En Route Automation Modernization, system was developed by Lockheed Martin. With ERAM, ARTCC controllers are able to track 1,900 aircraft at a time, an increase of 800 over the old Host system. Because the ERAM is designed to process data from almost three times as many radar sites, coverage extends beyond facility boundaries, enabling controllers to handle additional traffic more efficiently. Eventually the greater coverage will allow controllers to make use of a three-mile, rather than the current 5 mile, separation. ERAM also increases flexibility in routing around congested airspace, weather and other restrictions.

According to the FAA, the ERAM was designed with NextGen in mind. It will support satellite-based systems, such as Automatic Dependent Surveillance — Broadcast, and data communication technologies. This, in turn, will clear the way for future gains in efficiency and safety.

This next generation technology has the capability to determine exactly how closely an aircraft is following its flight plan, which will improve the efficiency of the ATC system. To do this, the system needs to know the sophistication level of each aircraft and the capabilities of the pilots using it. Conventional domestic flight plans do not have the extra fields that communicate this data to the ERAM, hence the use of the ICAO (International Civil Aviation Organization) flight plan. The equipment portion of the ICAO flight plan, plus the data entered in the "other information" field, identify the technological abilities of both the aircraft and the pilot.

Eventually most IFR flight plans will be required to use the ICAO form, but for now the FAA is slowly introducing its use. Domestic ICAO flight plans can be filed for RNAV Standard Instrument Departures (SIDS) and RNAV Standard Terminal Arrivals (STARS).

You do not have to file a domestic ICAO if you are simply flying an RNAV approach. To receive the preferential routings you must be on a STAR. Some pilots are confused by this. What's the difference? Look at the approach plates for Atlanta's Hartsfield-Jackson Airport. If you are assigned the RNAV(GPS) RWY 9R approach, you do not file an ICAO flight plan. You do file an ICAO flight plan for the CANUK SEVEN ARRIVAL

(RNAV). If it has a name, and says it is RNAV, then you should file ICAO.

By starting slowly, with one small segment of the aviation population, the FAA can field test the ability of the computers to accept the flight plans and "train" pilots and ATC personnel to think in terms of ICAO flight plans. At this time, because pilots are not strictly required to file ICAO in order to use the preferential RNAV SID and STAR routes, it is done only at the pilot's request.

ICAO flight plans are required for filing international flights out of the U.S. over water. Domestic flight plans are still used to fly to Canada and Mexico as long as the aircraft stays over land. Should you wish to file ICAO to any other country or over the oceans, Flight Service will transfer your calls to the flight service specialists who specialize in those flights, or you can reach an ICAO flight plan specialist directly by calling 1-800-432-4716. If you forget that number, call the usual number (1-800-wxbrief) and ask for southern Florida.

FLIGHT FOLLOWING

Last week I took a call from a pilot who wanted to file a VFR flight plan and get a standard briefing. I got to the AIRSPACE NOTAM section of the brief and was about to give him information on parachute jumping and unmanned rocket activity enroute when he stopped me and said "I don't need those, I'll be doing flight following and the Center will keep me away from them."

Houston, we have a problem. This pilot expressed a belief that Flight Following would give him all the same benefits as flying IFR but without the hassle of having ATC direct his every move. The reality is that VFR Flight Following can be very helpful to the pilots, but has its limitations.

The controller's bible, FAA Order 7110.65, and the Aeronautical Information Manual (AIM) both describe Flight Following as simply "Traffic Advisories". These Advisories are issued to alert pilots to other known or observed air traffic which may be in such proximity to the position or intended route of flight of their aircraft to warrant their attention.

The manuals go on to note that traffic advisory service will be provided to the extent possible depending on higher priority duties of the controller or other limitations; e.g., radar limitations, volume of traffic, frequency congestion, or IFR traffic workload. Traffic advisories do not relieve pilots of their responsibility to see and avoid other aircraft. Pilots are cautioned that there are many times when the controller is not able to give traffic advisories concerning all traffic in the aircraft's proximity; in other words, when a pilot requests or is receiving traffic advisories, he/she should not assume that all traffic will be issued.

ATC is not required to do VFR traffic advisories at all if their IFR traffic levels are high. If they do the advisories then the VFR aircraft will receive indications when there are other aircraft near their altitude. If someone is doing parachute jumping from 10,000 feet, and you are traveling at 6,500 feet, that is not traffic and may not be pointed out. The Center may know that there is parachute jumping scheduled in that area from sunrise to sunset, but the controller may not know which aircraft are pushing people out of the airplane at what precise moment. It is expected that all pilots, IFR and VFR have received NOTAM information prior to flight and are on the lookout. IFR traffic might be routed around the area, but VFR are not under direct control.

Same with Military Operating Areas. IFR traffic is not allowed into a MOA at all when they are active or expected to be active. VFR traffic can transit a MOA at their own risk. If he has time, a Center controller should mention when the MOA is occupied by F16's doing fighter practice maneuvers…but I've spoken to several pilots who were transiting the area and had the daylights scared out of them.

Another big concern should be the unmanned rocket NOTAMs. Unmanned aircraft should be treated by ATC the same that manned aircraft are – they have transponders and are being operated in a specific area – so you should get point outs. Unmanned rockets on the other hand do NOT have transponders. They are small and fast. Again, ATC controllers have access to the same NOTAMs that pilots do. They know that an area is expected to have rocket launches during a certain time period up to a predicted altitude. ATC cannot see the rockets on RADAR therefore they cannot point them out. ATC will direct IFR traffic around the area, but aircraft on VFR flight following are supposed to have gotten the NOTAMs and be doing their own navigation.

Something else that pilots using Flight Following should be aware of, once an aircraft is RADAR identified, squawking a discrete code and talking to ATC, they must not stop the service without telling ATC about it. If you are suddenly quiet and switch your transponder back to VFR, the controller is required to initiate search and rescue protocol as soon as he notices your Aircraft ID has disappeared from his scope.

If you are flying low enough, you may go out of radio communication – as soon as you notice this you must try to get hold of some other entity, like Flight Service, Flight Watch, etc... and ask them to contact the ATC facility you were speaking with to let them know you are all right, just no longer able to maintain contact. Should you be flying into an area where ATC knows their RADAR coverage will not extend down to your altitude, they will terminate the Flight Following.

Flight Following is very handy for VFR pilots as it helps to know where to look for other aircraft. It is not a substitute for knowing where there could be hazards along the route and planning accordingly. Be sure you know in advance all the things that could affect your flight enroute – get those NOTAMs for parachute jumping, pyrotechnic (fireworks) demonstrations, unmanned rockets, unmanned aircraft, balloon launches, so you can avoid them before they can become a problem.

ATC Zero!

In the summer of 2015 the act of an imbecilic, self-centered, vindictive twit caused the Chicago Air Route Traffic Control Center to shut down for awhile. The news media had all kinds of fun with that one. Yes, there was disruption to air traffic, mostly to the airports in and around Chicago itself, but the system did what it is designed to do and things came back online in a progressive and orderly fashion.

Every ATC facility – Center, Tower, Approach and Flight Service – is required to have a contingency plan in place that is reviewed annually, not just by the facility managers but by every supervisor and air traffic controller. Chicago ARTCC has high and low altitude sectors that abut other Center's airspaces. The first thing that happens when a facility becomes "ATC ZERO" is that the surrounding facilities are notified to implement the predetermined procedures. Notices to Airmen (NOTAM) are released by Flight Service concerning all affected airports and airspace so pilots planning flights in those are alerted to the situation and given guidance as to how to plan flights.

In this case, Minneapolis, Kansas City and Indianapolis Centers turned on their back up frequencies, extended their radar scopes outward in the sectors bordering Chicago Center so they could "see" into the neighboring airspace and started working Chicago's traffic. Chicago Approach control, and all other ATC facilities that exist under the dome of Chicago Center, still had all their frequencies and radars because their systems work independently.

An Air Route Traffic Control Center (ARTCC) is a very large building and the airspace designated as its responsibility is separated into many smaller blocks of sky. Since the damage done at the facility was not immediately catastrophic to the building as a whole, they were able to evacuate the personnel in an orderly manner and turn over control of those chucks of atmosphere to other ATC facilities before running out the door.

What was disrupted the most was the smooth and efficient flow of aircraft into and out of the area's major airports. Many smaller low altitude aircraft could choose to cancel their IFR flight plans and proceed VFR to their destinations. The aircraft traveling above the PCA were the ones turned over to other facilities…who worked them until they had exited the airspace or landed.

Of course the first thing that happens is a time period where all aircraft on the ground and in the air that would have entered the affected airspace were either ground stopped, rerouted or just slowed down until the initial redistribution of airspace goes into effect. Chicago is the 5th busiest Center in the country – but the airspace it controls is smaller than many of the others. It only has two major international airports - which are large enough that the flight delays provided the newscasters with lots of airtime. Anyone who was keeping an eye on the situation would have seen that it only took a couple of days for the airlines to get back on track.

For really large airports, flow control normally begins well outside the airspace of the Center which supports that airport. Aircraft landing Chicago are lined up 10 miles in trail beginning almost 500 miles away in several well organized streams. During the time the Center was closed, the feeder streams were diverted a little and ATC modified flight plans for high altitude aircraft to accommodate the new flow control procedures.

Historically there have been situations where power outages or disasters have caused the shut down of some towers and approach controls, but this was the first time a modern ARTCC actually went to ATC Zero. Past experiences with older facilities are what stimulated the incorporation of back up generators and radars and today's requirements for annual equipment and procedural reviews. The flying public can expect that this event will be studied in depth by the FAA, and that the experience will engender new ideas and requirements that will enhance the safety of all ATC facilities.

IFR Clearances

Many requirements for working with Air Traffic are similar whether you are talking to Flight Service, Tower, Approach or Center. One area that pilots are constantly questioning is what is expected and possible when obtaining a "Clearance".

A Clearance is an IFR option that VFR aircraft only encounter if they are transiting, departing or landing in an area whose high density of aircraft has created a requirement that all aircraft in that space must be talking to an Air Traffic Control facility. So for the purposes of this section we will concentrate on aircraft flying according to IFR rules.

What is a Clearance?

Every so often I get emails from pilots – both students and veterans – that want to clarify some point of aviation as related to air traffic that may be a bit cloudy when buried under the mountains of "government-eez" which makes up most of the FAA publications. Several emails have dealt with Clearances.

Essentially, a clearance means that ATC is going to keep all other aircraft who are flying under their control out of your way (Clears the area) as long as you are flying the routes and altitudes specified by the instructions you are given by the controller. You still have to keep an eye out for other VFR aircraft not talking to Air Traffic. If you are flying IFR your flight plan begins the negotiation process.

ATC attempts to meet your flight plan requests as closely as possible. Before giving you a clearance, ATC personnel look at the route you have requested in your flight plan to determine that the route/altitudes meet the safety needs of the area, and are not in conflict with other aircraft. The "clearance" is a verbal approval of your flight to be "as filed" in the flight plan, or if it needs to be changed they will issue instructions which allow you to reach your destination via another pathway in order to maintain safety and meet local restrictions.

Out west, where there are few airports and few aircraft competing for airspace, almost anything that a pilot files will be allowed. However, in areas like the east coast where everybody and his brother wants to fly in the same place at the same time, routings have been established for safety purposes. In this case if someone files direct from one point to another across those routings, ATC will issue clearances that require the aircraft to comply with those routes, altitudes and possibly speed restrictions.

Do VFR aircraft require clearances?

Pilots fly VFR because they want to be able to go anywhere they wish without having to ask permission all the time. However, there are places they must conform to ATC instructions due to traffic density or other restrictions.

IFR aircraft are on clearances from the time they depart to the time they land. VFR aircraft must also have clearances if they cross into or out of airspace that is under ATC control such as Approach Controls, or Tower airspaces. In this case, the VFR aircraft does not have to be on a flight plan, but they must be in contact with the ATC entity controlling that airspace prior to entering and follow their directions while in their territory.

VFR aircraft may want to depart or land an airport under controlled airspace, or they may simply want to transit the area. If they are entering the airspace to transit or land, then they should call ATC while still 5 to 10 minutes outside the area.

"Albuquerque Approach, Cessna 12345 is 20 miles east at ten thousand five hundred squawking 1200 landing Double Eagle airport...request clearance."

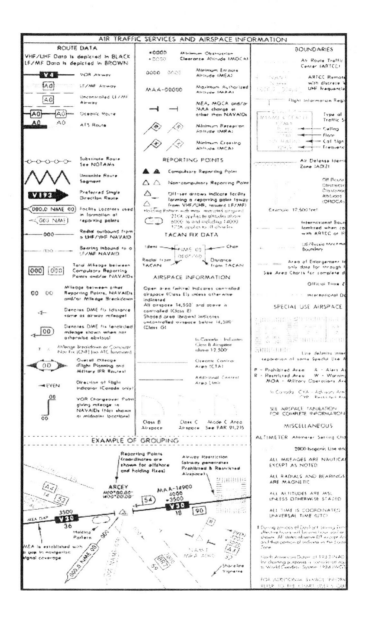

IFR Clearance Limits

Questions from Pilots

Hi Rose

I am a student pilot and a little confused about IFR clearance limits? If I am cleared to the NDB by my airport do I go to it and then continue on to my destination?

---Joyce

Hi Joyce,

Clearance limits can be NAVAIDs, intersections, other airports or in some cases recognizable physical landmarks – such as a power plant or race track.

When you are issued a clearance limit short of your destination it is because you are entering an area of high density traffic and ATC needs you to stay in place while they figure out a way to work you into the flow safely. The airspace from your departure airport to the clearance limit is held sterile of other IFR traffic until you appear on radar and are in contact with air traffic. Once you have come up on frequency and they can "see" you, they give you the rest of the clearance to your destination.

--Rose Marie

Hi Rose Marie

I have had many students ask me how long is a IFR clearance good for in hours? As an example can I get a clearance and then go back in the FBO and come out later and still have the IFR clearance valid? From the time I receive the clearance until I take off how long is this good for. I have delayed as much as an hour and things have worked. What is the FAA's take on this? I understand if I am issued a "void time" I would have to re-file a new flight plan.
--Gary

Greetings Gary,

The truth is that it varies by whether you are receiving the clearance from a towered airport or a small field with no ATC presence. If you receive the clearance from a Tower you are normally not actually cleared to depart - you are given the clearance routing, altitudes and frequencies, but are expected to get a separate taxi clearance to the runway and then wait for the Tower to clear you onto the runway then cleared to depart. That clearance should remain good until the flight plan expires.

When you are flying off of a small airport with no ATC on the field and you call for clearance from flight service, or in some instances from an approach control governing the airspace, the clearance contains all required data, releases you and clears you to depart the field. That clearance is good until the void time. The 7110.65 - the bible of air traffic - instructs controllers to issue void times of no more than half an hour, and I have seen them as short as 3 minutes. The airspace over your departure airport is held sterile until you have departed and are in contact with air traffic.

Some pilots, mostly small commercial aircraft, will call for a clearance well in advance of their planned departure time to get the route, altitude and frequencies, knowing that they will have a Hold For Release. They have the information but cannot depart until they call back and ask for a release. Once they call back they are given the release and the void time.

Of course, if other IFR traffic is inbound to their airport, ATC will not release them until after that aircraft cancels IFR or they have other confirmation that the inbound aircraft has landed.

If you are given a void time and you miss it, you do not have to file another flight plan, just call flight service or approach back and ask for another void time. The other elements of the clearance should still be good unless ATC changes it at that time. You only have to file a new flight plan if the one you are using times out. It will normally time out two hours after your proposed time of departure.

--Rose Marie

Dear Rose Marie,

"Several years ago I was an active CFII. As I recall it was not considered proper to request pop up clearances as routine. Having read your recent article I now wonder if it is considered proper to radio for an IFR clearance either from the ground or in the air?
Ted (Ohio)

Hi Ted,

If you can get Center or Approach on the ground and cut out Radio as the middle man, that is actually preferred. If you have to be airborne to get Center or Approach, but you can get Radio on the ground that is preferred.

If you are in an area where both are difficult, so you would have to call Flight service and get a clearance over the phone - that's when preference is iffy. There are times when getting a clearance by phone is absolutely necessary - such as when you simply cannot depart VFR.

You did not state what type of aircraft you fly, it makes a difference if you are slow and low versus high and fast. Pop up slow and low (C150, PA28, MO20, C210) are easier to maneuver into the flow of outbound traffic.

High and Fast (Lear, C500, CL60, etc...) demand to be worked in immediately. The High and Fast aircraft are frequently also needing to be worked into the Flow Control or Traffic Management system.

Should you feel a need to become airborne and do an IFR Pick up, you need to make sure that "IFR PU" is in the remarks of your flight plan. Center and Approach do not like IFR Pick ups unless necessary because they want to be able to talk to the pilot while he is still on the ground in order to work him into their traffic and keep from having conflicts with aircraft that may be inbound to the field you are departing.

As long as you can talk to anyone on the ground to get your clearance, go that route first. Although you are not supposed to use cell phones in the air, as an alternative, you could call on a cell phone from the aircraft while you are on the ground to the Flight Service Clearance Delivery phone number (1-888-766-8267) to get your clearance.

As you get the clearance make sure that Flight Service has the cell phone number in case they need to call you back. This makes good sense, especially if you have a Hold For Release from Center.

Have the Clearance Delivery Phone Number (1-888-766-8267) in your "phone book" - and remember to give the right state name - you can't get a clearance for Ohio if you say ANY when the system asks who you want to talk to and remember that calling the pilot briefing line may not get you to the correct facility to get a clearance at all.

(More about IFR Pop-Ups on P297!

NOTE from Rose:

Remember to always be an active participant in getting your clearance. If you are departing from a non-towered field and have to call flight service or an approach control, give them the alpha-numeric designation of the departure airport as well as the name of the town and state you are calling from. There have been numerous instances of confusion over the airport identification that have resulted in operational errors and could have resulted in accidents.

ATC wants the same information for the intended destination airport – so they can ensure that the flight plan they are clearing your aircraft with is the correct one. There have been instances where two pilots have filed totally different flight plans using the same call sign, usually in a situation where there are multiple users of the same aircraft.

If there is no frequency coverage on the airport grounds and you plan to use a cell phone to call for clearance, be sure that this is the number filed on your flight plan in case ATC or flight service needs to call you back. Sometimes cell phones will cut out in the middle of the clearance or towards the end – do not assume you have the entire clearance until you have read it back to ATC and they have stated "read back correct".

The author working on position at ABQ AFSS in 2007

What is a Special VFR Clearance?

The basic meaning of VFR or Visual Flight Rules is that an aircraft is only flying in areas where he can see and avoid aircraft or clouds or terrain/buildings…etc. The FAA determined that VFR aircraft should not fly when visibilities are below 3 miles laterally or 1,000 feet vertically because the closure rate between them and other aircraft/obstacles (2 to 4 miles a minute or more) may be more than they can pull out of in a tight situation. These are referred to as IFR conditions.

Say, however, an aircraft is flying in VFR or MVFR (marginal VFR — 5 miles visibility/3,000 feet) and wants to land or depart an airport in which the surface conditions are reported to be IFR. If that aircraft can see his way out of or to the airport, he can request Special VFR clearance. In this case he must stay clear of clouds as usual, but the ATC facility in charge of the area is ensuring that the other aircraft under their control will stay away and not come popping out of the clouds. In ATC parlance, the airspace is "cleared". Same if he simply wants to transit the area. In all cases the aircraft should contact ATC at least 5 minutes prior to entering the airspace for clearance "to", "through", or "out of."

ATC will ask him to squawk a code so the aircraft can be identified on radar, and once they "see" the aircraft they will give permission (clearance) for the aircraft to enter the airspace. Like with IFR aircraft they may include some instructions, though most of the time the only requirement is for the aircraft to remain clear of clouds while travelling the area.

Once the aircraft lands, departs, or is finished transiting the airspace they must inform ATC they are done. ATC "terminates radar services", tells the aircraft to squawk VFR (transponder code 1200) and the aircraft can go on their merry way.

Chapter 21

Understanding the Rules

Many of the articles I have written over the years contain information not specific to just one branch of ATC. Here are some which cover the finer details of clearance delivery, air traffic sequencing, charts, TFR's, traffic management and frequencies.

Airplane 54 Where Are You?????

Have you ever called for a pilot briefing, or to activate a VFR flight plan, or to get an IFR clearance, and found yourself confused as to where you were? It happens now and then – especially when a pilot has been flying for awhile, making multiple hops. I recall once while I was working at El Paso Flight Service, a tired looking man walked up to the briefing counter (remember those?), gave me his call sign then asked for a briefing to El Paso.

Amused, I looked at the disheveled young man and asked him if he knew where he was. He looked up startled and said "Midland?". When I told him he was in El Paso he shook his head and walked out.

A few minutes later another pilot came in. He gave me the same aircraft ID as the previous gentleman and asked for a briefing. Smiling, I asked him if he knew where he was.

When he looked at me strangely I relayed what had just occurred. He laughed and said, "Don't mind him, he's just the navigator!"

Mistakes in airport identification can also be made when pilots and flight service people do not communicate all the necessary data. This can have serious consequences to safety when an IFR clearance is involved.

Though the pilot and the flight service specialist are both supposed to ensure the identification of the departure and destination stations, frequently a pilot will call for clearance off of an airport, but not give the alphanumeric designation of that airport or the state. They may simply say "Off of Peru going to Columbus".

A specialist working the Great Lakes area clearance delivery line should verify that the pilot means Springfield, Indiana, not Springfield, Illinois by naming the three letter identifier as well as the state. This works most of the time, but only if the pilot knows the identifier.

At one time in the past a pilot called for clearance off of Grants, New Mexico. He did not give the three letter identifier. When the FSS specialist called ATC for a clearance there was no flight plan. The specialist relayed that information to the pilot, who was annoyed, and a new flight plan was put into the system quickly. Based on the pilot's request, the identifier for Grants (GNT) New Mexico was entered into the flight plan. ATC gave the specialist a clearance.

The Air Traffic center over Grant County, New Mexico airport was not happy when this aircraft popped up into their airspace.

Who was at fault? The pilot who said Grants instead of Grant County? Possibly. How about the specialist who did not announce the three letter ID of the airport? That may have triggered the pilot to realize something was wrong. The fact that the flight plan was not available to the ATC facility in control of that airspace should have given both of them pause.

Another reason to always use the alphanumeric lies in similar sounding airport names combined with crackly radios or cell phones. There are about 24 Farmington Airports in the U.S, and 15 Springfields. Some of these airports use the same frequency to request clearance from flight service – so it is not a given that the specialist working radio will automatically know which airport you must be departing if you just say Farmington.

The reason for stating the airport or town name in addition to the three letter identification is because the letter combinations are frequently similar within a given state. For instance, there are four airports in Alabama whose identifications are a combination of either Zero, eight and Alpha, or O, eight and alpha. (i.e.: A08, 08A) Zeros and O's are often confused.

It is wise to positively identify the destination airport as well so that when the specialist talks to the ATC facility controlling the airspace the correct flight plan is used. There have been instances where more than one flight plan was filed for an aircraft off of the same departure airport, but going to different destinations. Sometimes this is because two different pilots filed, or one flight plan was filed by a student and another by his instructor. Sometimes a pilot files using DUATS and an hour later decides to refile to a different destination without removing the first flight plan.

To ensure your safety, always state the alphanumeric identifier of the airports you are departing from and flying to as well as the airport or town name and the state. Positive communication only takes a moment, but it keeps us all out of trouble.

How Flight Plan Filing Affects Your Clearance

As an aircraft departs the earth IFR, it becomes part of a carefully choreographed process designed to facilitate safe and efficient movement through the crowded skies of the United States.

IFR Clearances can be very straightforward or they can take twists that pilots do not always expect. Strangely enough, the clearances that are the least confusing are those that are provided at large, busy airports. Simply study the standard instrument departures... it is rare that Clearance Delivery will give any other method of departing their airspace. Of course in any location with a tower, receiving your Clearance does not mean you have permission to taxi to the runway and take off. Clearance Delivery gives you the information about frequencies and departure procedures only. Ground Control and Tower take over from there.

Where there is no tower, clearances departing small to medium sized airports contain a number of variables depending on how the flight plan route was filed, what runway is in use, the local terrain and, on the coasts, what the normal flow is in congested areas. TFR's can also play a factor. In these locations, once you receive your clearance from ATC you are free to taxi to the runway and depart according to the instructions you receive in the clearance.

Controllers clear you "as filed" if at all possible. If there is any small element that ATC must change, they will read the entire routing to you – which may delay your departure as you frantically search through your charts to determine where you are required to fly.

Most pilots are familiar with those factors that affect their home airport, but many do not bother to check for variances at airports they plan to fly into. For instance, you can land and depart SRR (Sierra Blanca) airport in New Mexico from the east, north or south, but taking off to the west for general aviation or air carrier aircraft is forbidden. There is a mountain directly to the west, creating a physical barrier, and there is also a permanent Restricted area that extends from 50 miles northwest to 150 miles southwest of Sierra Blanca that is out of bounds. If you try to file SRR direct LAX you will normally be routed north to the CNX VORTAC.

That is the risk of filing direct – you never know what clearance you will receive. Investing some time in studying the normal routings for your flight and/or talking to other pilots in the area pays off in time and fuel saved. The allure of GPS direct can fool a pilot into believing he does not need to study IFR charts to get to his destination. Anyone familiar with flying a coast line – especially out east – knows that ALL aircraft are required to fly over specific routes and altitudes.

Computer Limitations

A pilot called Flight Service wanting to take off VFR from a small airport called Elizabethtown (EYF) and pick up an IFR clearance over the top of another, larger airport – Fayetteville, (FAY). As he filed the flight plan he wanted to show the identifier of the larger airport as his "departure point" on the flight plan. Unfortunately, if he had done so he may not have received the service he wanted.

To comprehend the problem requires an understanding of how the Air Route Traffic Control Center computers think. Center computers are programmed to hold your flight plan as a proposal in the main computer bank until half an hour prior to flight time. At that point, the proposal "pops up" at the sector or tower it expects you to contact for clearance. It does not generate any other data at any other station until after the flight plan is activated.

If the pilot had entered FAY as his departure point, the computer would send his proposal to only one place – the clearance delivery position at Fayetteville Tower. Since he planned to be above FL090 as he crossed over the airport, FAY Approach Control would have been the location that needed the proposal.

The pilot thought that filing the departure as FAY instead of KFAY would take care of that problem – but it does not. The "K" indicates an airport instead of a NAVAID to pilots and controllers, the computer does not recognize the difference. This is one of the reasons why the FAA has been systematically changing the identifiers of VORTACs and other NAVAIDs located near major airports...(ie, RNO, Reno Nevada's VORTAC was changed to FMG, Mustang).

To remedy the pilot's situation was simple-choose a radial/DME off of the FAY VOR as his departure point. Even if the Radial/DME is just the same as the location of the airport reference the VORTAC, the computer will recognize that the location is not on the ground at the airport. A Radial/DME causes the computer to assume the identifier refers to the NAVAID rather than the airport. Flight Service used the FAY078010. The proposal for the flight plan was routed to the correct Approach Control position awaiting activation. Of course the pilot came on frequency as he entered Approach airspace and they were ready for him.

There are other tricks to filing IFR pop-ups. Using the identifiers of small airports that do not have towers will send the flight plan to the correct

ARTCC or Approach sector - so will using NAVAIDS, latitude/longitudes, or intersections.

When you file an IFR Pop-up be sure to put IFR PUP in the remarks of the flight plan, and always tell your briefer to add those remarks when filing with Flight Service. This alerts the controlling facility to the fact that you will be already airborne when you contact them.

Another possibility for misunderstanding comes when you plan to make a practice approach at several airports enroute. This is not really a problem for low flying aircraft – if your altitudes are within Approach airspace, the Center computer will generate notification to Approach that you are transiting their airspace. By adding the contraction PLA (Practice Low Approach) and the name of the airport in remarks cues the controllers to your intent. (Example: PLA BWG)

However, if you filed an altitude above the level of any approach control or tower airspace enroute, the controllers at the approach control will not be expecting you, and the Center will not know you need a clearance to descend. For example, ABQ Approach monitors the airspace within a 30 nautical mile radius, surface to 17,000 feet. If you have filed IFR at FL180 or above and want to do a practice approach at ABQ before going on to your destination, ABQ will not have access to your flight plan and the Center will not know you plan to descend until you make a request.

The most practical method of handling the situation is to file multiple flight plans. This is not hard to do, once the first one has been filed, all you need to do is change a few items. The Center computer recognizes where you need to take off and land, so it sends the flight plan inbound and proposal to the right place, the Center controllers recognize your need to descend and will work you into their traffic pattern, and the towers at those airports will be expecting you. Again, be sure to put PLA in remarks on the flight plan and on initial call up tell the approach controller if you do not intend to land, because you will need to be given the clearance to your next stop as you are lining up for the approach.

If there is no approach control your next leg will begin at that airport, so as you contact the Tower inbound, tell the Tower controller how many approaches you would like to make, and when you are done you would like your clearance on to the next airport. When the controller gives you the next clearance, you will receive a new squawk code. The first flight plan is closed by the computer as you land, and the next one is activated as the computer picks up the new squawk.

A note about flight plans. IFR flight plans are automatically closed if you land at a towered airport. If your destination does not have a tower – you must either close the flight plan with ATC airborne or call flight service immediately upon landing.

VIP TFR

FDC 6/7201 ZDC SECURITY...SPECIAL SECURITY
INSTRUCTIONS, WASHINGTON, DC.
THIS NOTAM AND COMPLEMENTARY NOTAMS REPLACE FDC
6/6468 TO PROVIDE UPDATED INSTRUCTIONS. THIS NOTAM
REFERENCES THE WASHINGTON DC SPECIAL FLIGHT RULES
AREA (SFRA) ONLY. A SEPARATE NOTAM REFERENCES THE
WASHINGTON DC FLIGHT RESTRICTED ZONE (FRZ)
PROCEDURES AND OPERATIONS BY UNMANNED AIRCRAFT
SYSTEMS (UAS), INCLUDING MODEL AIRCRAFT (HOBBYIST OR
RECREATIONAL USA ONLY), CIVIL AND COMMERCIAL
OPERATIONS, AND PUBLIC OPERATIONS WITHIN THE SFRA.
SPECIAL SECURITY INSTRUCTIONS FOR AIRCRAFT
OPERATIONS IN THE DC SFRA ARE IN EFFECT PURSUANT TO
14 CODE OF FEDERAL REGULATIONS (CFR) SECTIONS 93.335,
93.337, 93.339, 93.341, 93.343, 93.345, AND 99.7, AND 49
UNITED STATES CODE (USC) SECTION 40103(B)(3). THIS
NOTAM AND THREE RELATED NOTAMS REGARDING THE: DC
FLIGHT RESTRICTED ZONE (FRZ); LEESBURG MANEUVERING
AREA (LMA); AND UNMANNED AIRCRAFT SYSTEM (UAS)
OPERATIONS IN THE DC SFRA CLARIFY AND SUPPLEMENT THE
OPERATING REQUIREMENTS PRESCRIBED BY THE CITED 14
CFR SECTIONS. SECTION I. RESPONSE AND ENFORCEMENT:
PURSUANT TO 49 USC 40103(B)(3), THE FAA HAS
ESTABLISHED THE DC SFRA AS 'NATIONAL DEFENSE
AIRSPACE'. PERSONS WHO DO NOT ADHERE TO THE

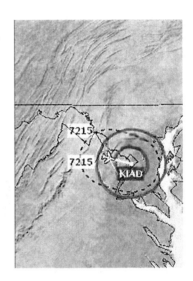

The graphic seen here is from the AFSS.com PilotWeb site. When your route of flight has been entered in the pilot briefing tool you can open the TFR Tab and see whether or not your route of flight intersects a current TFR. This is valuable as it gives you a chance to figure out if you are going to need a re-route before you fly. The text to the left describes the area and the restrictions associated with it in greater detail. If you have problems interpreting it, just call flight service.

TFRs – An Airspace Shell Game

It's that time of the decade again…politicians abound, bouncing from place to place across the country, usually getting in everyone's way while spouting their messages of discontent. Whether you root for Republicans, dig the Democrats or (like me) lean towards the Libertarians, you have got to keep at least three flight levels ahead of them if you don't want to be caught in their jetwash.

The FAA tries to give you as much information about political movements as possible with Temporary Flight Restrictions (TFR's). You can expect them whenever the seated President or Vice-President is on the move, and once all the teams have selected their quarterbacks you will see them popping up to protect airspace around them as well.

Any TFR restricts certain aircraft from flying within specific areas. These areas are defined both geographically and by altitude. For instance, a TFR that is issued for a forest fire may restrict all aircraft from flying within a 10 mile radius of a navaid, such as a VORTAC, or Latitude/Longitude (L/L) point, or if the area is particularly large, a series of radial/DMEs or L/L points may be used to define it. The TFR will also contain an altitude from the surface upwards which may be defined as either MSL or AGL. Aircraft must fly over it or around it.

The TFRs are issued according to specifications in the Code of Federal Regulations. If you look it up, find 14 CFR. Each type of TFR relates to a different section of that document. Some of them have exceptions to the rule, as with a forest fire TFR where the pilot's home base is within the restricted area, but you have to thoroughly read the section of 14 CFR that is specified in the TFR to determine if it allows any exceptions.

A Presidential TFR, also known as a VIP TFR is more complicated, and pilots in those areas are monitored intensely. It is issued several days in advance and effective throughout the Presidential visit. (Though frequently the news media knows about the events which engender them before we get the official TFR)

A VIP Temporary Flight Restriction (TFR) is transmitted to all Air Traffic Control facilities and online to those websites that serve the aviation community. The TFR describes concentric circles around wherever the President is planning to be. Typically, the outer circle may be a radius from 10 to 30 miles wherein all aircraft flying below 18,000 feet must be in contact with Air Traffic Control and identified on radar. Aircraft can still land and depart from airports located in that area. You must be on a VFR or IFR flight plan, and a transponder code is required.

The inner circle is usually a 10 mile radius wherein only specific aircraft are allowed to fly at all, usually military, police and emergency medical flights, and scheduled air carriers. Any airport existing inside that 10 mile radius is restricted from any other activity by civilian aircraft.

In other words, if you are flying on an airline, your landing or departure will be delayed while the president is physically at the airport, but once he leaves you will be allowed to continue. However, say you wanted to hop into your private plane and get your currency, or fly up to Aunt Mabel's place, until the TFR is lifted you will not be allowed to leave or arrive at that airport – or any other airport within the tenmile boundary. This also applies to part 135 air taxis and package haulers. For example, let us assume Air Force One were to land at Phoenix International, and then the President was driven to a hotel 5 miles east where he was to stay during the course of his visit. For whatever length of time he was there, no unauthorized aircraft would be allowed to land or depart from the airports located at Mesa, Stellar, Williams or Chandler airports, as well as Phoenix itself.

TFR's issued for the Vice-President and white house hopefuls are much smaller, usually a 3 nautical mile radius below 3,000 AGL. Unfortunately, these grandstanding politicos tend to be bodies in motion – and the TFR's move with them – if they land and do a bus or train tour – the TFR's get very complicated. The Lockheed Martin pilot briefers receive daily updates on these movements and have maps showing which airports are affected.

If you are planning any future flights you can access the official TFR information through WWW.TFR.FAA.GOV. The information is arranged by the city and state closest to the TFR and the type of TFR it is. Presidential TFRs are listed under VIP. If you click on a listing, the computer will bring up a map and dialogue concerning when and where pilots are not allowed to fly. If you access the list, you can limit the list by clicking on TYPE and then selecting VIP from the dropdown list.

Under the map there is a link called "sectional chart" which shows the boundaries in more detail including what airports will be affected. The information concerning Time periods in a Presidential TFR are written in both Universal Coordinated Time (UTC) and in local time using the 24 hour clock.

Keeping track of the VIP TFR's will ensure you don't get caught in a situation where you are either trapped on the ground or trapped outside of your home base, and for sure you don't want to deal with FSDO for a TFR violation!

Where Does It Say I Can't Fly There?!

Before a flight, every pilot knows he is responsible for discovering what conditions he will encounter during his time in the air. He is supposed to investigate the current and forecast weather, the Notices to Airmen related to his destination airports and any Temporary Flight Restrictions or airspace hazards he may encounter along his chosen route.

When pilots call Flight Service to get a standard briefing, it includes the Notices to Airmen...but many pilots seem to think that Flight Service is responsible for giving them more than that. Recently I know of a VFR pilot who flew blithely through an active Restricted Area. When he landed and the FSDO inspector came to ask why, his answer was that Flight Service did not tell him it was hot during his briefing. He seemed surprised to discover that although Pilot Briefs do include NOTAMs that are put out reference any Special Use Airspace, the Briefer is not tasked with researching the FAA's Published Data concerning that airspace.

All Special Use Airspace (SUA) areas are depicted on Sectionals and VFR charts with a list as to the times that the airspace is normally in use. NOTAMs are only put into the system for times that are outside the norm. Some SUA's are only active by NOTAM, so you must check the current NOTAMs for those, but in general a Pilot Briefer will only look up the regularly scheduled times if that information is specifically requested by a pilot.

Some FDC NOTAMs have been around for so long that pilots either forget about them or just don't realize that they are still in effect. There are airspace restrictions around the big theme parks like Disneyland, and an ongoing restriction that is a coverall for all major outdoor events. Do not fly within 3000 feet AGL and three miles laterally of ANY stadium, racetrack, amphitheater or any other place where thousands of people are likely to gather. This includes high school and college football games. It is natural to be curious about why the lights are blazing somewhere below you, but consider them a warning to stay away, not a beacon to your curiosity. If someone has binoculars and catches your tail number as you swoop overhead, they could report you to FSDO.

There are many other more specific informational items that are not included during the NOTAM portion of a pilot weather briefing. Data that is published well in advance for major sporting events – like the Indianapolis 500, or airshows like Oshkosh is not researched for every briefing. There may be related NOTAMs at the airports in the area regarding runway closures or Airspace activities, but the many and myriad details of the event must be researched in the FAA's published NOTICES TO AIRMEN. This document is updated monthly and is available online at http://www.faa.gov/air_traffic/publications/notices.

The NOTICES TO AIRMEN document contains FDC data related to changes in airports, facilities and airspace procedures, International Flight Prohibitions and potentially hostile situations, Oceanic Airspace Notes, and information related to Sporting and Entertainment events, such as NASCAR races and the Albuquerque International Balloon Fiesta.

The cover page of the document states "Notices to Airmen included in this publication are given during pilot briefings unless specifically requested by the pilot."

MOA (Military Operating Areas) are not closed to VFR traffic (though IFR will be always be routed around or over them) however, you are transiting at your own risk. It is best to contact the ARTCC controlling that airspace and asking if the area is hot or not. Many MOAs are scheduled active every day, but they may not contain aircraft for the entire time. If you call the Center frequency in that area as you travel towards it, they will know if it is currently active or if it will go active within half an hour.

It is confusing that the FAA uses the same terminology for both NOTAMs that are Published and known about for months in advance and those informational NOTAMs that come up suddenly and may be active for a very short time. Flight Service can find any information you need, but if it is in a published document, it will not be part of a standard Pilot Briefing. If you have a specific SUA or TFR in mind, you can ask them to check on it.

GPS Satellites

GPS Anomalies

You are flying along at about 12,000 feet on a beautiful clear day in southwestern Utah. Your GPS shows you to be around St. George, and you are flying east to Albuquerque. You glance at your GPS and it gives you a reading in Mexico! Then a few minutes later it flickers and the reading is correct again. You think, "What in blue blazes is going on?!"

Before you smack the thing or make plans to take it to the repair shop, you might want to call flight service radio and ask if there are any GPS NOTAMs in the area.

For quite some time there have been NOTAMs put out by the Air Route Traffic Control Centers (ARTCC) dealing with the GPS system being "unreliable or unavailable" for set periods of time. This type of NOTAM recently began appearing in the Midwest around St. Louis as well.

When self briefing, using tools from online services or the FAA Web site, these NOTAMs are difficult to interpret because they are centered on a latitude/longitude (L/L). Most of them do not mention any NAVAID. As a result, in order for someone to understand whether or not it will affect his or her flight, the pilot must dial the L/L into a computer or GPS. Pilots who are in a hurry may not take the time to do this and the scenario listed above is the result.

Whenever Flight Service sees one of these NOTAMS on the "D" or Distant NOTAM list, they make sure all the briefers are aware of what's happening and how large an area it will cover. If you are briefing yourself, the GPS NOTAMs are a little tricky to find and interpret. They are located with the other "D" NOTAMs, usually at the bottom of the last page, and will be listed with an ARTCC identifier such as ZAB (Albuquerque Center) or ZKC (Kansas City).

Here is the text of a recent GPS NOTAM where the Lat/Long is based thirty-nine miles east of Truth or Consequences, New Mexico (TCS):

!GPS 02/026 (KZAB A0025/15) ZAB NAV (WSMR GPS 15-02) GPS (INCLUDING WAAS, GBAS, AND ADS-B) MAY NOT BE AVAILABLE WITHIN A 499NM RADIUS CENTERED AT 332339N1063058W (TCS 070039) FL400-UNL DECREASING IN AREA WITH A DECREASE IN ALTITUDE DEFINED AS: 454NM RADIUS AT FL250, 385NM RADIUS AT 10000FT, 378NM RADIUS AT 4000FT AGL, 366NM RADIUS AT 50FT AGL. DLY 1830-2230 1602111830-1602122230

Notice that the area described is an inverted cone. The higher you are flying, the larger the coverage area, which is why NOTAM was put out by Albuquerque Center. If you plot it out, at the highest altitude this NOTAM covers all of New Mexico, Arizona, Colorado, and parts of Utah, Nevada, Oklahoma, Texas and Kansas at FL400. At 50 FT AGL it still covers a 366 nautical mile radius of the TCS area.

These NOTAMs are issued by every ARTCC whose airspace is touched during the exercise, and most of them are for specific hours of the day for a set period of time. The bulk of them are centered near military ranges or bases such as White Sands in New Mexico, Davis Monthan AFB area in Tucson, AZ and other locations in southern Utah and Nevada. However you can also see them occasionally in other areas, most recently St. Louis.

One way to know if the GPS is acting wonky is to keep half an eye on the old-fashioned navigational equipment just to see if the readouts agree.

Having the sectional around so you can glance to see if the railroad tracks are where they should be is helpful too.

The other type of NOTAM that you will see frequently concerning GPS is one that says GPS 24 PRN OTS. This means that the pseudo random noise generator on GPS satellite number 24 is out. Why is this important?

The PRN functions like a kind of lens that focuses the signal being broadcast from the satellite. When it is not functioning correctly the signal from that satellite may be fuzzy and off by several miles. When this NOTAM shows up and if your brand of GPS receiver allows it, you should remove that satellite from the ones it is receiving. If you cannot remove it, then it usually won't make a lot of difference for VFR and most IFR navigation as long as your receiver is picking up at least three other satellites because your GPS equipment should collate all the various signals it receives into the position display. Where it may make a difference is where pinpoint navigation is really important – like on some IFR approaches.

In this era of aviation navigation the GPS has become the instrument of choice for most pilots. Be aware of any outages in the system before you take to the sky so you end up in the right place!

Stay on Top of the Charts!

A series of incidents over the past few years has illuminated a potentially dangerous trend. An accident in Los Alamos, New Mexico, an incident near Belen, and a potential for disaster at Albuquerque exist because the pilots involved used old aviation charts and AFDs.

Let's face it, buying a whole new set of charts and AFDs every few months is downright expensive and for the most part 99% of the information remains the same. It's the changes that can kill you. Nonetheless, I have heard of pilots who are using charts that are a decade or more old.

A few years ago two Bonanza V-tails were landing at Los Alamos, New Mexico. Both of them broadcast their intentions on CTAF. One of them was using non-current charts containing old frequency information. They lined up to land on the same runway. In a maneuver so perfect it could never be repeated, one landed right on top of the other.

Fortunately the story ends well. The pilot on the bottom did not realize anything was amiss until he looked out his window and saw a wheel. The pilot on the top thought he was awfully high up to have landed and come to a stop. Neither was injured, though it took a crane to lift the one on top from the cradle of the V-tail on the bottom.

In another incident, an FAA Airways Facilities Technician based in Albuquerque was flying his friend's Citabria. He had all the latest charts and was landing at his home base of Belen just south of Albuquerque. As it was getting dark, he turned on his landing lights, broadcast on UNICOM and was lined up on final. Just after touchdown he looked ahead and saw an Aerostar (no landing lights on) touching down at the other end of the runway headed right for him.

Quickly, he slowed and pulled off the runway into the dirt as the Twin blew past him. He saw the other pilot in the FBO. The other pilot had called on an old UNICOM frequency listed on his out of date charts and was rude enough to not even apologize for his nearly disastrous incompetence.

In December of 2008, a new ATC tower opened at Double Eagle Airport (AEG) on the west side of Albuquerque. The new tower's frequency was 118.3. Almost immediately, problems began to occur because up until nearly four years previously the frequency for the tower at Albuquerque International (ABQ) was 118.3.

Pilots with old charts were calling Albuquerque Tower on 118.3 and getting the new tower and since both airports are in Albuquerque, the new tower controllers had to determine where the pilots really want to land before issuing a clearance. The FAA realized the potential for disaster and changed the frequency for Double Eagle Tower.

The FAA charts are your best bet for the most current information. If your charts are not current and you want to check on the frequencies, ask your pilot weather briefer. Flight service specialists have current information at their fingertips that takes just a few minutes to pull up.

Some of the aviation websites contain good information but they are not always current. A month after the ATC tower at AEG was opened, I visited two of my favorite websites: www.airnav.com and www.flightcentral.net. At that time neither of them had updated the websites to include the new data. I did email the information to both of them.

Although current issues of the FAA Airport Facility Directories are available online from the FAA (Google AFD), the site pulls up whatever information was printed at last issuance and any changes will not appear until the next printing. The AFD information on new towers is only available in the national NOTAM database until that time.

The Flight Service PilotWeb site,   https://lmfsweb.afss.com offers pilots some of the FAA's publications including AFD and approach plates online. These are free along with the ability to file flight plans and receive weather information.

So use your old charts for something useful – like gift wrapping paper. Incidents like the ones listed above are avoidable. If you can afford to fly, you can afford to fly responsibly. Stay current and stay alive.

Small Drone – under 55 pounds

Military Drone – as large as a fighter jet.

Watch out for Drones!

The skies are no longer solely populated by birds and pilots. The number of unmanned aircraft and unmanned rockets being launched is increasing daily and the FAA is in the position of trying to create new regulations to govern them.

One problem is that many of the people guiding these machines do not even know there are regulations they should be following. Dads buy their kids the biggest, fanciest remote control aircraft they can get at a hobby store or online for Christmas. Many of those will not threaten private aircraft because they cannot get more than 200 feet off the ground, but what happens when the individuals are flying them close to the approach end of a runway? Many realtors these days are paying to have a drone with a camera mounted on the bottom fly over expensive properties so they can post the images on their website. Others are using that same technology to harass the rich and famous. These drones are flying at altitudes that some helicopters fly.

Because many UAS drones are fitted with cameras, they are challenging the privacy of everyone. One operator in Kentucky thought it was fun to hover over the teenage girl sunbathing in her backyard – right up until her father shot the drone. When he tried to sue the father, the judge ruled that his act was an invasion of the girl's privacy. Obviously the courts are going to be busy with developing new privacy laws to accommodate America's latest pastime.

There are amateur rocket groups sending their inventions well up into the flight levels. The vast majority of them have waivers, and put out the appropriate NOTAMs before their flights. What of the backyard inventor who doesn't bother to find out about regulations?

Additionally we have universities doing research into alternate applications for unmanned aircraft – like crop-dusting. One major shipping company has requested that the FAA allow them to use drones to deliver packages in major cities. Can you see them zipping around office buildings and landing on the rooftops?

These are all concerns that the FAA is addressing. Their website (https://www.faa.gov/uas) defines how unmanned air vehicles are classified and what current requirements and restrictions are in effect at this time. Model aircraft owners can be fined if they fly too close to airports or over 500 feet AGL.

The government separates UAS into three categories: Public (government), Private (commercial), and Hobby. Public and Private must have waivers, file NOTAMs and meet stringent controls. Hobby UAS are required to be less than 55 pounds, not used for commercial purposes, and always within visual range of the operator, they are not required to file NOTAMs as long as they meet the Hobby restrictions.

Right now the only way pilots can watch out for these activities is by checking the AIRSPACE NOTAMs during a preflight briefing. Many times pilots doing self briefs will look at the NOTAMs at the departure and destination airports, but skip lightly over the ones enroute. In addition to unmanned aircraft and rockets, AIRSPACE NOTAMs give you data on fireworks (PYROTECHNICS), airshows, aerobatic aircraft and Parachute

320

jumping.   Be aware of what can happen — look hard at AIRSPACE NOTAM.

So many Unmanned Aircraft NOTAMs are now in effect daily that Flight Service has developed a graphics display of their locations.   Preflight Briefing Specialists can overlay an aircraft's route to see how close they will come to these areas.   The same data is available on the Flight Service *PilotWeb* site.   Input minimal flight plan information and ask it for a briefing then look for the tab labeled UOA (UAS Operating Area).   Try using the TUS area in your route of flight to see some relatively permanent UAS test sites.   Most UAS sites along a route are depicted, and those NOTAMs that are not are listed on the page.

General Aviation pilots everywhere should do their best to keep on top of developments in this arena.   VFR uncontrolled airspace is precious and already being reduced or eliminated in many parts of the country with the growth of TRACON's, restricted areas and prohibited areas.   Sharing that airspace with a machine being operated from an unknown distance can be disturbing.   Know what is happening and ensure your flying future by feeding your opinions and data to those lawmakers governing our skies.

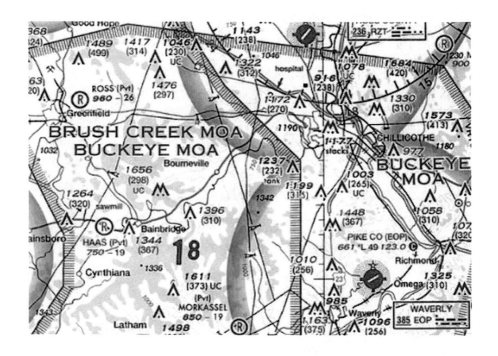

Military Operating Areas (MOAs) are just one type of Special Use Airspace it is best to avoid when active!

Special Use Airspace

Before our military aviators can fly out into the fray, conquering the enemy and carrying the day, they have to have three things: An aircraft, training, and practice. The kind of training and practice, of course, depends on what the aircraft is designed to do. To this end there are many forms of Special Use Airspace (SUA) across the nation, each dedicated to a different purpose.

In the past, the military would call either the Center or Flight Service and create NOTAMs for general aviation to disseminate. Most of these would show up when a pilot requested a flight briefing alongside the other NOTAMs enroute such as aerobatics areas and NAVAID outages. Recently there has been a change in how the NOTAM information is created, which may make them more difficult to find if you are attempting to self-brief online.

First of all, NOTAMs are only created for the SUA areas that are not published, or are being used outside of published times. If the SUA is listed on the sectionals, IFR charts and VFR charts with time periods, it does not appear as a NOTAM in a briefing. If they are published, but the effective time reads "by NOTAM", they are the areas which will appear under NOTAM criteria in a briefing or online when active.

There are several types of Special Use Airspace. When Restricted Areas are hot, no aircraft is authorized inside. Period. Many of these, such as R5107B over White Sands Missile Range may be permanently "HOT". Others of the R5107 series may only be hot when the military is testing weapons – a really good time to avoid the area!

Military Operating Areas (MOA) are primarily used for combat and aerobatic flight training and although VFR general aviation aircraft may enter them while in use, it is not advised. IFR aircraft must be routed around active MOA's. Unlike Restricted areas, a MOA may be scheduled active Monday through Friday sunrise to sunset, for example, but it will not be in continuous use during that time. The Air Route Traffic Control Center computer generates a flight plan strip or message to the sector which controls that MOA half an hour prior to the time an aircraft will occupy the airspace. When that aircraft comes on frequency he is cleared into the area, and when he plans to leave the area he must get clearance to leave it. The only way to determine if the area will be in use is to call the Center as you approach the area.

Alert Areas are also open to general aviation and is airspace which may contain a high volume of pilot training activities or an unusual type of aerial activity, of a level the military does not consider to be hazardous to aircraft.

Prohibited Areas, like Restricted areas, are in continuous use and closed to aircraft penetration. Most of these are non-military use areas that require a high level of security, such as research laboratories, Camp David, or ex-presidents' homes. NOTAMs for these are issued when the area is created and numbered, and left as a NOTAM until the information is published, then the NOTAM is cancelled.

Military Training Routes, or MTRs are broken down into Visual routes (VR), Instrument routes (IR) and Slow Routes (SR). They are designed to teach pilots how to navigate and fly with stealth over various types of terrain. Many of them enter and exit MOA's to allow pilots to simulate approaches into enemy territory, engage the enemy, then leave the area. Some MTR's allow for high speed aircraft at low altitudes, so be aware of these route locations!

The most recent changes to the NOTAM issuance involve Aerial refueling tracks (AR) and Night Vision Goggle (NVG) training. Flight Service used to publish all NOTAMs for this activity, and the information would show up along the route of flight with all other parachute jumping and aerobatic area NOTAMs. The military changed the requirements so that only the air refueling activity occurring in a non-published area, and NVG activity taking place outside of MOAs have NOTAMs issued by Flight Service. Information about active times of published AR tracks and NVG in MOA areas is published by the Centers.

This means that when a pilot is self-briefing online using DUATS or other pilot websites, the SUA information displayed in the long list of NOTAMs may be in different sections. Information which is disseminated by Flight Service has a location identifier attached which keys it to the route of flight. In most systems the NOTAMs enroute are listed from departure to destination in a fashion that most closely follows the route. A NOTAM for unpublished aerial refueling may be a third of the way through the list.

Most of the NOTAMs published by a Center are grouped together, normally at the bottom of the list. This is where you should look for the active times of published SUA's. Be aware that some pilot briefing websites will not show the NOTAMs that are published by the Centers. The most accurate list of NOTAMs available on the web is through the FAA's website.

https://pilotweb.nas.faa.gov/PilotWeb. This site allows you type in a single location or a Center address and get all the associated NOTAMs. Type in ZAB (Albuquerque Center) sometime – quite a list!

The FAA requires Flight Service to provide NOTAMs concerning Restricted Areas, Aerial Refueling, and Night Vision Goggles during a standard briefing. All other SUA information is available upon request.

Our military pilots are talented and well trained, but a Cessna taking a short cut through a MOA while some F16's are practicing dog fight maneuvers may be hard to resist. (WE HAVE A BOGEY!) If you aren't carrying extra underwear, check those SUA NOTAMS!

STMP

Using the Special Traffic Management Programs

The plane is warmed up, you've got the weather and it is supposed to be a beautiful sunny day with no adverse conditions. So you hop in your Twin and fly up to Eagle, Colorado eager to shush your way down a mountain. Then you call the tower – and they refuse to let you land!

Unfortunately a lot of pilots do not realize that most of the ski airports around the country require reservations during certain times of the year. This is also the case for those airports supporting large sporting events such as the World Series, the Master's Tournament, College Bowl Games, and the Superbowl. STMP's are sometimes issued for airports serving events like the Sturgis motorcycle rally, or large airshows and fly-ins. (DUH)

If the event is taking place near a city, not only the major airport, but all the surrounding smaller airports may be included in the STMP program. So if you are heading to Indianapolis for the Brickyard 400, do not assume that you can land at Greenwood (HFY), or Eagle Creek (EYE) without an STMP reservation!

Though most large airports have daily traffic management procedures, the Special Traffic Management Programs or STMP's are implemented when a special need exists. Let's go back to the ski areas.

The Aspen (ASE), Eagle (EGE), and Rifle (RIL), Colorado airports, the Hailey/Sun Valley (SUN), and Twin Falls (TWF) airports of Idaho and the Jackson Hole (JAC) airport in Wyoming all serve the most popular ski resorts in the Rocky Mountains. These airports are not continuously busy year round, so ATC may be minimally represented. For instance, Rifle has no tower and Eagle has only a VFR tower in operation. But let the flakes start flying and all these airports start running out of parking space quickly.

Believe it or not, that is one of the reasons for an STMP – ramp space. Frequently the ramps will be full at Eagle or Aspen, so only those aircraft dropping passengers off, then leaving quickly, will be allowed to land.

STMP's provide spacing for aircraft entering airports with difficult landing conditions – which in the case of Aspen, Eagle or Rifle can mean any time – even clear days. Toss in icy runways and a pilot will really enjoy knowing that he can take his time without being pressured by the guy behind him.

Do you know when the ski areas are the busiest? Easter week. Mexico takes Easter very seriously – most of the businesses in the country close down for a week. As a result, hundreds of executive jets sporting an "X" in their tail number flock north for a last chance ski weekend before spring seriously sets in.

The current rules regarding STMPs are:

- Reservations can be obtained beginning 72 hours in advance of the proposed operation.
- Reservations must be confirmed beginning 24 hours *but no less than* 12 hours prior to the proposed operation or the reservation will be <u>automatically canceled</u> and made available to others seeking slot reservations.
- Reservations obtained within 24 hours of the proposed operation will be confirmed automatically.

- Only 2 reservations per request are authorized.
- Reservations may be made online or by phone.

Pilots should be prepared to provide their destination/departure airports, estimated date and time of arrival in UTC, call sign and type aircraft. You will be issued a preliminary reservation number, which will be changed to a confirmation number when you call back within 12 to 24 hours prior to your flight.

You must include your confirmation number in the remarks section of your flight plan. If you cannot make the window of time you have reserved, you may have to deal with extensive airborne holding or a reroute to an alternate destination. Aircraft are expected to arrive within 10 minutes (+/-) of their filed ETA.

The FAA requests that if you discover you cannot use a reservation, that you cancel it as soon as possible so another pilot may use it.

Flight Service is not allowed to get reservations for you, but you can easily access the STMP information through the FAA's website: http://www.fly.faa.gov/estmp/index.html. If you forget all that, just enter STMP into Google and it comes up at the top of the search list.

If you still stubbornly refuse to enter the computer age, you can call for a reservation at 1-800-875-9755. The Aeronautical Information Manual has a section on how to use the telephone interface.

Special Traffic Management Programs (STMPs) are implemented for special events that attract thousands of people and aircraft to participating airports. To properly manage the flow of arrivals and departures for these events, the FAA requires users to make arrival and departure reservations to and from these airports. This Web interface has been developed to simplify the reservation process and allow for more reservation flexibility.

When Systems Don't Work

Have you ever tried to tune into a frequency, a VOR, an ILS or an NDB only to have no response? Have you gotten strange readings from your GPS or WAAS? What do you do when this happens? Who should you report it to? The easy answer, and the most often correct one, is to report it to ATC. Let's take each one individually.

The steps ATC takes ensures that the component being reported is actually the culprit rather than the equipment in the aircraft. If it is a frequency or NAVAID, ATC will ask another aircraft to tune into the same frequency to verify that it is truly malfunctioning. If that aircraft is picking it up, then ATC will inform the initial reporting aircraft so that the pilot can have his equipment checked upon landing.

If you are tuned into an ATC frequency and no one answers, do not immediately assume any equipment is broken – Towers, Centers and Flight Service are frequently listening to more than one frequency and may be busy with another contact. Wait a few minutes, and then try your call again. If there is still no joy, go to another frequency which should work in your area and see if you hear anything.

If you are able to contact another ATC facility or use UNICOM to talk to an airport manager, have them call the ATC facility with the non-operational frequency and report it. Take a note of the time, your location, and the frequency and when you land call Flight Service to confirm they received the report. They will follow up on the information. They may also give you an alternate frequency so you can request the service you initially wanted to receive.

In general if the component in question is a NAVAID, it is best to call it in to Flight Service. If it is an ILS or other piece of equipment directly linked to an airport, report it to the tower or the airport manager. Flight Service can also take those reports if airport operations and towers have closed for the night. The FAA requires that all malfunctions are reported and repair records kept. Of course, NOTAMs are issued to warn other pilots of the problem.

Should you find a GPS or WAAS anomaly, report it immediately to the closest ATC facility. They will need the following information: Aircraft call sign and type, location, altitude and date/time of the occurrence. ATC notifies the military installation monitoring the GPS system and broadcasts the information to other aircraft in the area.

One of the most common problems with frequencies is the use of outdated charts, especially as concerns UNICOM frequencies. There have been several incidents of accidents wherein one of the two pilots landing on the same runway was using an old chart and was therefore broadcasting his position on a frequency no longer in use.

The most amazing example of this was at Los Alamos (LAM) airport in New Mexico where two V-tail bonanzas were landing. In a move that could never have been rehearsed they lined up for the runway with one directly above the other – and landed that way. There were no injuries. One pilot was reported to have said "I never knew there was a problem until I looked out my side window and saw a wheel."

There are always alternatives – use 121.5 if you have to, it was created for emergencies and not having a correct frequency, or having one dysfunctional can be an emergency when you need to be in contact with ATC. The specialist who responds can direct you to the correct frequency in your area.

The men and women of the Airways Facilities arm of the FAA work hard to keep all the equipment working, but they need you to let them know when it isn't.

References

FAA Orders:

JO 7110.65   Air Traffic Control

JO 7110.10   Flight Services

JO 7930.2   Notices to Airmen

JO 7340.2   Contractions

JO 7900.5   Surface Weather Reporting

Aeronautical Information Manual

Pilot Controller Glossary

AC 00-45G - Aviation Weather Services

www.afss.com

www.faa.gov

http://www.srh.noaa.gov/jetstream/tstorms/windshear.htm

About the Author

Rose Marie Kern entered the Air Traffic Control Academy in 1983. Since that time she has worked in the Center, Tower and Flight Service options. She has been writing articles about all facets of Air Traffic Control since 2004.

A member of the EAA, AOPA and the NM Pilot's Association, Rose is a popular speaker for aviation events. Her next book, *After the Strike*, is a memoir about what it was like for a single mother to enter the world of ATC while it was in the process of rebuilding, and while harassment laws were still more of a concept than a reality. It will be available in early 2017.

More information about Rose Marie, her books and links to more great information about ATC and aviation weather are available on her website: www.rosemariekern.com.

CPSIA information can be obtained
at www.ICGtesting.com
Printed in the USA
FFOW02n0006230117
31587FF